FAST
desserts

THE AUSTRALIAN
Women's Weekly

FAST
desserts

contents

It's good for our well-being that many of the best "fast" desserts call for fruit as their hero ingredient: any sense of guilt about consuming a sweet is tempered with the knowledge that it comes accompanied with healthy vitamins, antioxidants and fibre. Of course, chocolate, cream and sugar also loom large in the fast dessert equation but don't beat yourself up for occasionally eating just for pleasure. There are positive benefits, which also contribute to your well-being, that come from allowing yourself a decadent treat once in a while. Remember: all things in moderation, including indulgence. What these desserts do have in common, however, is that they are all great tasting and neither difficult nor time-consuming to make. Some of the fruit dessert recipes call for seasonal produce so plan to make them when the individual fruit is at peak quality and lowest price: try not to substitute canned fruit for fresh. The other ingredients are either already in your fridge or pantry, or readily available at your local supermarket. Quick and deliciously achievable, these sweet treats are the perfect end to a great meal.

fruit

Summer berry stack

450g brioche loaf
250g strawberries, sliced thickly
150g raspberries
150g blueberries
1 tablespoon icing sugar
blackberry coulis
300g frozen blackberries
¼ cup (40g) icing sugar
¼ cup (60ml) water

1 Make blackberry coulis.
2 Meanwhile, cut 12 x 1cm-thick slices from brioche loaf; using 7cm cutter, cut one round from each slice.
3 Combine berries in medium bowl.
4 Place one brioche round on each of four plates; divide a third of the berries among rounds. Place another round on top of each stack; divide half of the remaining berries among stacks. Place remaining brioche rounds on berry stacks; top with remaining berries. Pour coulis over stacks; dust each with sifted icing sugar.
blackberry coulis stir ingredients in medium saucepan over high heat; bring to a boil. Reduce heat, simmer 3 minutes. Strain coulis into medium jug; cool 10 minutes.

on the table in 25 minutes
serves 4

Sticky pears

40g butter
4 medium pears (920g), peeled, halved lengthways
1/3 cup (75g) firmly packed brown sugar
1 teaspoon ground cardamom
2 tablespoons green ginger wine
2/3 cup (160ml) double cream

1 Heat butter in large heavy-base frying pan; cook pear, sugar, cardamom and wine over high heat, stirring occasionally, about 5 minutes or until pears are browned.
2 Serve hot pears with cream.

on the table in 20 minutes
serves 4

Fruit skewers with honey yogurt

½ medium pineapple (625g)
2 large oranges (600g)
250g strawberries
2 large bananas (460g)
30g butter
¼ cup (55g) firmly packed brown sugar
1 tablespoon lemon juice
1 cup (280g) honey yogurt

1 Peel pineapple; cut away and discard core. Cut pineapple into 2.5cm lengths; cut lengths crossways into 3cm pieces. Peel oranges; separate orange segments. Remove hulls from strawberries; cut in half crossways. Peel bananas; cut into 3cm slices.
2 Thread fruit, alternating varieties, onto 12 skewers; place on oven tray.
3 Stir butter, sugar and juice in small saucepan over low heat until butter melts and sugar dissolves. Pour butter mixture over skewers, making sure that all fruits are coated in mixture.
4 Cook skewers, in batches, on heated lightly greased grill plate (or grill or barbecue) about 5 minutes or until browned lightly.
5 Serve skewers with yogurt.

on the table in 35 minutes
serves 4
tip you need 12 long bamboo skewers for this recipe; soak them in water for about 1 hour before using to avoid them splintering or scorching.

Mixed berries with sponge fingers

12 savoiardi sponge finger biscuits
1 cup (250ml) cranberry juice
400g french vanilla frûche
150g fresh raspberries
150g fresh blueberries

1 Dip biscuits in juice; divide among four 1½-cup (375ml) serving glasses. Sprinkle remaining juice over biscuits.
2 Divide half of the frûche mixture among glasses; sprinkle with half of the berries. Repeat layering with remaining frûche and remaining berries.

on the table in 15 minutes
serves 4
tip this dessert can be prepared several hours in advance; store, covered, in refrigerator.

Caramelised oranges with ice-cream

4 large oranges (1.2kg)
2 tablespoons brown sugar
2 tablespoons Grand Marnier
200ml vanilla ice-cream

1 Preheat grill.
2 Peel oranges, removing as much white pith as possible; cut crossways into thick slices.
3 Place orange, in single layer, on oven tray. Sprinkle with sugar; drizzle with liqueur. Cook orange on both sides under grill until just caramelised.
4 Divide ice-cream and orange among four serving dishes; drizzle with pan juices.

on the table in 20 minutes
serves 4
tip Cointreau or Triple Sec can be substituted for Grand Marnier.

Pineapple with coconut

1 small pineapple (800g)
⅓ cup (80ml) passionfruit pulp
2 tablespoons Malibu
¼ cup (10g) flaked coconut, toasted

1 Peel, core and thinly slice pineapple.
2 Divide pineapple among four serving dishes; drizzle with passionfruit and Malibu, then sprinkle with coconut.

on the table in 15 minutes
serves 4
tip we used Malibu in this recipe, but you can use any coconut-flavoured liqueur you prefer.

Baked rhubarb with gingernut ice-cream

800g trimmed rhubarb
⅔ cup (150g) caster sugar
4 (50g) gingernut biscuits, chopped coarsely
500ml vanilla ice-cream

1 Preheat oven to 200°C/180°C fan-forced.
2 Cut rhubarb into 8cm lengths. Place rhubarb into large, shallow baking dish in a single layer. Add sugar; toss gently. Bake, covered, 15 minutes. Uncover, bake further 5 minutes or until rhubarb is soft and sauce is syrupy.
3 Meanwhile, gently and quickly combine biscuits and ice-cream in medium bowl. Serve warm rhubarb with ice-cream and any syrup.

on the table in 35 minutes
serves 4

Nectarines on brioche

4 medium nectarines (680g)
40g butter, chopped
¼ cup (55g) firmly packed brown sugar
¼ teaspoon ground nutmeg
200g mascarpone cheese
1 tablespoon icing sugar
1 tablespoon Cointreau
2 teaspoons finely grated orange rind
2 small brioche (200g)
2 teaspoons icing sugar, extra

1 Halve nectarines; remove seeds, cut each half into thirds.
2 Melt butter in medium frying pan; stir in sugar and nutmeg until sugar dissolves. Add nectarines; cook, stirring, until browned lightly.
3 Meanwhile, combine cheese, icing sugar, liqueur and rind in small bowl. Cut each brioche into four slices; toast until browned lightly both sides.
4 Divide brioche slices among serving plates; top with mascarpone mixture and nectarine pieces. Dust with extra sifted icing sugar.

on the table in 20 minutes
serves 4
tip Cointreau is a clear orange-flavoured brandy.

Blackberry clafoutis

2 teaspoons caster sugar
1 cup (150g) frozen blackberries
⅓ cup (80ml) milk
⅔ cup (160ml) fresh cream
1 teaspoon vanilla extract
4 eggs
½ cup (110g) caster sugar, extra
1 tablespoon plain flour
1 tablespoon icing sugar

1 Preheat oven to 180°C/160°C fan-forced. Grease four shallow ovenproof dishes (¾ cup/180ml capacity); sprinkle inside of dishes with caster sugar. Divide blackberries evenly among dishes.
2 Bring milk, cream and vanilla to a boil in small saucepan. Remove pan from heat. Strain milk mixture through fine sieve into medium heatproof jug.
3 Whisk eggs and extra sugar in small bowl until creamy. Whisk in flour and strained milk mixture; pour over blackberries in dishes. Place dishes on an oven tray.
4 Bake about 20 minutes or until browned and set.
5 Serve warm, dusted with sifted icing sugar.

on the table in 35 minutes
serves 4

Melon salad with lime syrup

¼ medium watermelon (1.5kg)
½ large rockmelon (1.3kg)
½ large honeydew melon (900g)
lime syrup
⅓ cup (75g) firmly packed brown sugar
2 teaspoons finely grated lime rind
¼ cup (60ml) lime juice
⅓ cup (80ml) water

1 Make lime syrup.
2 Meanwhile, remove skin and seeds from melons, cut into chunks.
Combine melons with lime syrup in large bowl, toss to coat in syrup.
lime syrup stir ingredients in small saucepan over low heat until sugar
dissolves; cool 15 minutes.

on the table in 35 minutes
serves 4

Grilled bananas with vanilla cream

4 medium bananas (800g), halved lengthways
¼ cup (55g) firmly packed brown sugar
20g butter
2 tablespoons Malibu
1 vanilla bean
⅔ cup (160ml) thickened cream
1 tablespoon icing sugar

1 Preheat grill.
2 Sprinkle banana with 1 tablespoon of the brown sugar; place under hot grill until browned lightly.
3 Meanwhile, stir remaining brown sugar, butter and liqueur in small saucepan over low heat until smooth.
4 Split vanilla bean in half lengthways, scrape seeds into small bowl; discard pod. Add cream and icing sugar; beat with electric mixer until soft peaks form.
5 Serve banana with vanilla cream; drizzle with sauce.

on the table in 20 minutes
serves 4
tip we used Malibu in this recipe, but you can use any coconut-flavoured liqueur you prefer.

Pears with coffee syrup

4 medium ripe pears (920g)
½ cup (110g) caster sugar
2 cups (500ml) water
2 teaspoons instant coffee powder
4 squares dark eating chocolate
500ml vanilla ice-cream

1 Peel pears and cut in half crossways.
2 Stir sugar and the water in medium saucepan over medium heat until sugar is dissolved. Add pears; simmer, covered, about 10 minutes or until pears are tender. Remove pears from syrup.
3 Return 1 cup (250ml) of the syrup to pan; stir in coffee powder until dissolved.
4 Reassemble pears in serving bowls. Serve coffee syrup with pears, chocolate and ice cream.

on the table in 20 minutes
serves 4

Honey grilled plums and figs

8 small plums, halved, seeded
6 medium figs (360g), halved
⅓ cup (120g) honey
¼ cup (55g) firmly packed brown sugar
⅔ cup (190g) thick greek-style yogurt

1 Preheat grill.
2 Place plums and figs cut-side up in shallow, flameproof baking dish. Drizzle with half of the honey; sprinkle with sugar.
3 Cook fruit under hot grill until browned lightly and just tender.
4 Divide among serving plates, drizzle with remaining honey and juices from pan. Serve with yogurt.

on the table in 15 minutes
serves 4
tip make the most of plums and figs while they are in season. During winter months, you could use canned pears as a substitute.

Cinnamon toast with caramelised apples

4 large apples (800g)
60g butter
½ cup (110g) firmly packed brown sugar
¼ cup (60ml) water
¼ teaspoon ground cinnamon
300ml thick cream
8 slices cinnamon and fruit bread
30g butter, extra
1 tablespoon cinnamon sugar

1 Peel apples and remove cores; cut apple into thin slices.
2 Melt butter in large frying pan; cook brown sugar and the water about 5 minutes or until mixture boils and thickens. Add apple; cook until just tender. Stir in cinnamon and ½ cup (125ml) of the cream; return mixture to a boil.
3 Meanwhile, toast bread; spread one side with extra butter then sprinkle with cinnamon sugar.
4 Serve toast with apple mixture and remaining cream.

on the table in 15 minutes
serves 4

Apricot and almond crumbles

825g can apricot halves in natural juice
1 tablespoon brandy
½ cup (75g) self-raising flour
¾ teaspoon ground ginger
¼ cup (30g) almond meal
¼ cup (50g) firmly packed brown sugar
¼ cup (55g) caster sugar
90g butter, chopped

1 Preheat oven to 200°C/180°C fan-forced.
2 Drain apricots over small jug or bowl; reserve ½ cup (125ml) juice.
3 Slice apricots and divide among six ¾ cup (180ml) ovenproof dishes; place dishes on an oven tray. Pour combined brandy and reserved juice over apricots.
4 Sift flour and ginger into medium bowl; stir in almond and sugars, then rub in butter with fingertips. Sprinkle mixture over fruit.
5 Bake, uncovered, about 25 minutes or until browned. Serve hot with ice-cream or cream, if desired.

on the table in 35 minutes
serves 6

Strawberry croissant french toast

8 mini croissants
1 tablespoon strawberry jam
250g strawberries, sliced
1 tablespoon caster sugar
1 egg
¼ cup (60ml) milk
¼ teaspoon vanilla bean paste
40g butter

1 Preheat oven to 150°C/130°C fan-forced.
2 Using sharp knife, carefully cut open inside edge of croissants to make a pocket, leaving 1cm at each end. Spread jam in pocket and fill with strawberries.
3 Combine sugar, egg, milk and vanilla in large bowl.
4 Heat half of the butter in large frying pan over medium heat. When butter is sizzling, dip four filled croissants in milk mixture. Place croissants in pan and cook until golden brown on both sides. Remove from pan, place on wire rack over baking tray. Place in oven to keep warm.
5 Repeat with remaining butter, croissants and milk mixture.
6 Serve croissants dusted with sifted icing sugar and with extra strawberries, if desired.

on the table in 30 minutes
serves 4
tip substitute vanilla extract for vanilla bean paste, if you prefer.

Cherry and almond creams

400g cherries, pitted
½ cup (110g) caster sugar
2 tablespoons amaretto liqueur
250g light spreadable cream cheese blend
2 egg whites
4 Parisienne Langue de Chat biscuits for serving

1 Combine cherries in large bowl with 1 tablespoon of the sugar and
1 tablespoon of the amaretto. Stand 10 minutes.
2 Meanwhile, combine cream cheese with 2 tablespoons of the sugar
and remaining amaretto in small bowl until smooth.
3 Beat egg whites in small bowl with electric mixer until soft peaks form.
Gradually add remaining sugar, beating until sugar is dissolved between
additions; fold into cream cheese mixture.
4 Divide cherries among four 1½-cup (375ml) serving glasses. Top with
cream cheese mixture. Serve with the biscuits.

on the table in 25 minutes
serves 4

Caramelised peaches with spiced yogurt

6 medium peaches (900g), peeled, halved, seeded
¼ cup (55g) firmly packed brown sugar
spiced yogurt
¾ cup (210g) yogurt
¼ teaspoon ground cinnamon
¼ teaspoon ground cardamom

1 Make spiced yogurt.
2 Cook peaches on heated oiled barbecue grill plate until browned. Sprinkle with sugar; cook, turning, until sugar dissolves and starts to bubble.
3 Serve with spiced yogurt.
spiced yogurt combine ingredients in small bowl.

on the table in 35 minutes
serves 4

Plums with sour cream

825g can plums in syrup, drained
½ cup (120g) sour cream
½ cup (140g) honey yogurt
⅓ cup (75g) firmly packed brown sugar

1 Preheat grill.
2 Halve plums; discard seeds. Divide plums among four 1-cup (250ml) shallow flameproof serving dishes.
3 Combine sour cream, yogurt and 2 tablespoons of the sugar in small bowl. Spoon sour cream mixture over plums; sprinkle with remaining sugar. Place under grill about 3 minutes or until sugar caramelises.

on the table in 15 minutes
serves 4

Strawberries dipped in lavender honey toffee

440g (2 cups) raw sugar
125ml (½ cup) lavender honey
60ml (¼ cup) water
1.25kg strawberries

1 Stir sugar, honey and the water in small saucepan over low heat until sugar dissolves. Bring to a boil, boil about 5 minutes or until golden brown (or hard crack stage on a sugar thermometer).
2 Place a strawberry on the end of a wooden skewer and quickly dip two-thirds of the strawberry into the toffee.
3 Place strawberry on baking-paper-lined oven tray, gently remove skewer. Repeat with remaining strawberries. If toffee becomes too firm while dipping, return pan to low heat until toffee melts.

on the table in 20 minutes
serves 10
tip you can find lavender honey (produced by bees fed on lavender) at selected delicatessens. If unavailable, any variety of honey can be used.

Red fruit salad with lemon mascarpone

1kg seedless watermelon
250g strawberries, quartered
150g raspberries
2 medium plums (225g), sliced thinly
1 tablespoon caster sugar
⅓ cup (80ml) kirsch
lemon mascarpone
250g mascarpone cheese
2 teaspoons finely grated lemon rind
2 teaspoons caster sugar
1 tablespoon lemon juice

1 Make lemon mascarpone.
2 Cut watermelon into bite-sized pieces.
3 Place watermelon pieces in large serving bowl with strawberries, raspberries, plums, sugar and liqueur; toss gently to combine. Cover; refrigerate until ready to serve.
4 Serve fruit salad with lemon mascarpone.
lemon mascarpone combine ingredients in small bowl.

on the table in 20 minutes
serves 4
tip use a melon baller to scoop watermelon into bite-sized balls, if desired, for a more decorative look.

Grilled bananas with malibu syrup

4 large ripe bananas (920g)
⅓ cup (80ml) maple syrup
2 tablespoons Malibu
¼ cup (15g) shredded coconut, toasted

1 Split bananas lengthways. Combine maple syrup and liqueur; brush about a quarter of the mixture over the cut-sides of bananas.
2 Cook bananas, cut-side down, on heated lightly oiled grill plate (or grill or barbecue) until lightly browned and heated through.
3 Serve bananas while hot, drizzled with warmed remaining syrup and toasted coconut.

on the table in 15 minutes
serves 4
tip we used Malibu in this recipe, but you can use any coconut-flavoured liqueur you prefer.

Panettone with ricotta cheese and caramelised peaches

3 medium peaches (450g)
⅓ cup (75g) firmly packed brown sugar
2 teaspoons amaretto liqueur
2 x 100g panettone
1 cup (200g) ricotta cheese

1 Cut each peach into eight wedges. Cook peach and sugar in large frying pan about 5 minutes or until sugar dissolves. Reduce heat, simmer, uncovered, about 10 minutes or until peach is soft and pan juices are syrupy. Gently stir in liqueur.
2 Meanwhile, slice each panettone crossways into six pieces; toast panettone lightly both sides.
3 Divide panettone among serving plates; top with cheese and peach, drizzle with pan juices.

on the table in 25 minutes
serves 6
tips if small panettone are unavailable, cut 7cm rounds from large panettone, brioche or fruit bread. Amaretto, originally from Italy, is an almond-flavoured liqueur and can be purchased from liquor stores.

Berries with warm white chocolate sauce

½ cup (125ml) cream
125g white eating chocolate, chopped finely
1 tablespoon Malibu
500g strawberries, quartered
300g blueberries

1 Bring cream to a boil in medium saucepan; remove from heat.
Add chocolate; stir until smooth. Stir in liqueur.
2 Serve warm sauce over berries.

on the table in 15 minutes
serves 4
tip we used Malibu in this recipe, but you can use any coconut-flavoured
liqueur you prefer.

Pineapple crunch

850g can crushed pineapple, drained
2 small nashis (360g), chopped coarsely
1 tablespoon Malibu
3 cups (150g) Just Right
2 tablespoons pepitas
2 tablespoons sunflower seeds
⅓ cup (95g) yogurt
2 tablespoons honey

1 Preheat oven to 180°C/160°C. Grease four 1-cup (250ml) ovenproof dishes; place on oven tray.
2 Combine fruit and liqueur in medium bowl; divide among dishes.
3 Using one hand, crumble cereal in same medium bowl; stir in seeds, yogurt and honey. Divide mixture among dishes; bake, uncovered, 20 minutes or until browned lightly.

on the table 30 minutes
serves 4
tips you can substitute chopped, drained canned peaches or apricots for the pineapple in this recipe. We used Malibu in this recipe, but you can use any coconut-flavoured liqueur you prefer. We used Just Right breakfast cereal in this recipe but you can use any flake and dried fruit cereal, even a muesli or granola-like product.

Caramelised pear bruschetta

⅓ cup (80ml) thickened cream
1 cup (200g) ricotta cheese
¼ cup (45g) finely chopped crystallised ginger
1 tablespoon icing sugar
6 corella pears (900g)
60g butter
⅓ cup (75g) firmly packed brown sugar
¼ cup (60ml) orange juice
2 small brioche (200g)

1 Beat cream in small bowl with electric mixer until soft peaks form; fold in cheese, ginger and icing sugar.
2 Cut each pear into eight wedges; remove and discard core and peel.
3 Melt half of the butter in large frying pan; cook pear, stirring occasionally, until browned lightly. Add remaining butter and brown sugar; cook, stirring, until pear just starts to caramelise. Add juice; cook, stirring, 1 minute.
4 Meanwhile, cut each brioche into four equal slices; toast until browned lightly both sides. Divide brioche slices among serving plates; top with cheese mixture then caramelised pear.

on the table in 20 minutes
serves 4

Brandy snaps with strawberries and cream

125g packaged cream cheese, softened
2 tablespoons icing sugar
1 tablespoon Grand Marnier
½ cup (125ml) thickened cream, whipped lightly
6 large strawberries
8 brandy snap biscuits
2 tablespoons passionfruit pulp

1 Beat cream cheese, icing sugar and liqueur in small bowl with electric mixer until smooth. Fold in cream.
2 Slice four of the strawberries and cut remaining two in half.
3 Place one biscuit on each serving plate; divide half of the cream cheese mixture among biscuits, top each with sliced strawberries.
4 Top with remaining biscuits, remaining cream cheese mixture, halved strawberries and passionfruit.

on the table in 10 minutes
serves 4
tips you will need two large passionfruit for this recipe. Cointreau can be substituted for Grand Marnier.

62

Summer fruit in blackcurrant syrup

1 vanilla bean
½ cup (125ml) water
1½ cups (375ml) blackcurrant syrup
4 medium apricots (200g), halved, stoned
4 medium plums (450g), halved, stoned
2 medium nectarines (340g), halved, stoned
2 medium peaches (300g), halved, stoned
200g french vanilla frûche

1 Split vanilla bean in half lengthways; scrape seeds into medium saucepan. Add pod, the water and syrup to pan; bring to a boil. Boil about 5 minutes or until syrup thickens slightly.
2 Add fruit, reduce heat; simmer, turning fruit occasionally, about 8 minutes or until fruit is tender. Remove from heat; discard vanilla bean. Serve fruit and syrup topped with frûche.

on the table in 30 minutes
serves 4

Grilled nectarines with passionfruit yogurt

8 medium nectarines (1.3kg), halved, seeded
2 tablespoons brown sugar
1 tablespoon Grand Marnier
1 cup (280g) yogurt
2 tablespoons icing sugar
2 tablespoons passionfruit pulp

1 Preheat grill.
2 Place nectarines, cut-side up, on a baking tray or dish; sprinkle with sugar and liqueur. Place under grill until nectarines are browned.
3 Meanwhile, combine yogurt and sugar in medium bowl; spoon into serving bowl, swirl with passionfruit pulp.
4 Serve nectarines with passionfruit yogurt.

on the table in 20 minutes
serves 4
tip Cointreau or Triple Sec can be substituted for Grand Marnier.

Char-grilled fruit

½ medium pineapple (600g)
2 medium mangoes (860g)
½ cup (125ml) Malibu
¼ cup (60ml) passionfruit pulp
1 tablespoon brown sugar
300ml thickened cream, whipped
2 tablespoons flaked coconut, toasted

1 Remove and discard top and base from pineapple. Cut pineapple into 1cm-thick slices; cut each slice in half. Cut mangoes down each side of stone; cut a criss-cross pattern into flesh.
2 Combine Malibu, passionfruit pulp and sugar in small saucepan. Stir over low heat, without boiling, until sugar dissolves. Simmer, uncovered, 5 minutes. Combine fruit with passionfruit syrup in large bowl.
3 Cook fruit, on heated oiled barbecue, until browned both sides and tender, brushing occasionally with some of the syrup during cooking.
4 Drizzle warm fruit with remaining passionfruit syrup. Serve with cream; sprinkle with coconut.

on the table in 35 minutes
serves 4
tips you will need about 3 passionfruit for this recipe. We used Malibu for this recipe, but you can use any coconut-flavoured liqueur you prefer.

Winter fruits and lemon grass grilled with a palm sugar and star anise syrup

½ cup (125ml) red wine
1 vanilla bean, halved lengthways
¾ cup (200g) finely chopped palm sugar
⅔ cup (160ml) water
¼ cup thinly sliced fresh lemon grass
6 star anise
6 small pears (1kg)
4 small bananas (520g), halved
2 large red grapefruit (1kg), peeled, sliced thickly
2 large oranges (600g), peeled, sliced thickly

1 Stir wine, vanilla bean, sugar, the water, lemon grass and anise in small saucepan until sugar dissolves.
2 Add pears (pan needs to be small enough for pears to stand upright and close together); simmer, uncovered, about 15 minutes or until pears are just tender. Remove pears from pan; bring syrup to a boil. Simmer, uncovered, until syrup has reduced by half.
3 Meanwhile, preheat grill.
4 Place pears, banana, grapefruit and orange in large baking dish; drizzle with a little syrup. Place under hot grill about 5 minutes or until fruit is lightly browned. Serve fruit drizzled with remaining syrup.

on the table in 35 minutes
serves 6
tips we used two pear varieties, corella and beurre bosc as well as ladyfinger bananas, which are shorter and sweeter than the better-known Cavendish variety. Either type of banana can be used.

Balsamic strawberries

500g strawberries, quartered
2 tablespoons balsamic vinegar
⅓ cup (55g) icing sugar
⅓ cup (80g) crème fraîche

1 Combine strawberries, vinegar and sugar in medium bowl; stand 25 minutes.
2 Divide strawberry mixture among serving dishes, top with crème fraîche.

on the table in 35 minutes
serves 4
tip strawberries can also be served with light sour cream or yogurt.

Caramelised figs with spiced yogurt

1 cup (280g) yogurt
¼ cup (35g) roasted pistachio nuts, chopped coarsely
¼ teaspoon ground nutmeg
1 tablespoon caster sugar
6 large fresh figs (480g)
1 tablespoon honey

1 Combine yogurt, nuts, nutmeg and sugar in small bowl.
2 Halve figs lengthways. Brush cut-side of figs with honey.
3 Cook figs, cut-side down, in heated oiled large frying pan 5 minutes.
Turn figs; cook further 5 minutes or until browned lightly.
4 Serve figs with spiced yogurt.

on the table in 20 minutes
serves 4

Grilled fruit kebabs with passionfruit sauce

½ cup (125ml) water
¼ cup (60ml) orange juice
½ cup (110g) caster sugar
1 tablespoon honey
½ cup (125ml) passionfruit pulp
2 tablespoons Cointreau
1 small pineapple (800g), chopped coarsely
1 small papaya (650g), chopped coarsely
2 large bananas (460g), sliced thickly
250g strawberries

1 Stir the water, juice, sugar and honey in small saucepan over heat, without boiling, until sugar dissolves. Bring to a boil. Reduce heat, simmer, uncovered, without stirring, about 8 minutes or until mixture thickens slightly. Remove from heat; stir in passionfruit pulp and liqueur. Cool 5 minutes.
2 Thread fruit onto skewers; brush with passionfruit sauce. Cook kebabs on heated oiled grill plate (or grill or barbecue) until browned lightly, brushing occasionally with passionfruit sauce.
3 Serve kebabs drizzled with remaining passionfruit sauce.

on the table in 35 minutes
serves 4
tips you need about 6 passionfruit for this recipe, as well as 8 skewers. If using bamboo skewers, soak them in water for about 1 hour before using to avoid them splintering or scorching. We used Cointreau in our sauce, but you can use Triple Sec, Grand Marnier or any orange-flavoured liqueur you prefer; you can also choose to use no alcohol at all.

Melon and pineapple with honey lime syrup

⅓ cup (120g) honey
½ cup (125ml) lime juice
400g fresh pineapple pieces
400g fresh honeydew melon pieces
200g honey yogurt

1 Combine honey and juice in small saucepan, bring to a boil; simmer, uncovered, 5 minutes.
2 Place pineapple and melon in large bowl add honey mixture; toss gently to combine.
3 Serve fruit mixture with yogurt.

on the table in 15 minutes
serves 4

Toffeed mandarins with ice-cream

50g butter
⅓ cup (75g) firmly packed brown sugar
5 medium mandarins (1kg), peeled, segmented
1 litre vanilla ice-cream

1 Melt butter in large frying pan; cook sugar and mandarins, stirring, until sugar dissolves and mandarins soften slightly.
2 Divide ice-cream among serving bowls; top with mandarin mixture.

on the table in 20 minutes
serves 4

Poached pears with chocolate cream

4 medium ripe pears (920g), peeled
1 litre (4 cups) water
1 cinnamon stick
1 vanilla bean, halved lengthways
½ cup (110g) caster sugar
200g dark eating chocolate, chopped
½ cup (125ml) cream

1 Place pears, the water, cinnamon, vanilla and sugar in medium saucepan; cook, stirring, over medium heat until sugar is dissolved. Bring to a boil. Simmer, covered, about 8 minutes or until pears are just tender, drain.
2 Meanwhile, stir chocolate and cream in small saucepan over low heat about 5 minutes or until smooth.
3 Pour chocolate cream over pears to serve; add a scoop of vanilla ice-cream, if desired.

on the table in 30 minutes
serves 4
tip canned halved pears can be substituted for fresh pears to save time.

Banana and coconut cream parfait

¾ cup (180ml) thickened cream
2 tablespoons icing sugar
2 tablespoons Malibu
300ml mango coconut crème ice-cream
4 large bananas (920g), sliced thinly
½ cup (25g) flaked coconut, toasted

1 Beat cream, icing sugar and liqueur in small bowl with electric mixer until soft peaks form.
2 Layer ice-cream, bananas, coconut and cream mixture in four 1½-cup (375ml) serving glasses.

on the table in 15 minutes
serves 4
tip we used Malibu in this recipe, but you can use any coconut-flavoured liqueur you prefer.

Berries with orange syrup and mascarpone cheese

2 egg whites
250g mascarpone cheese
120g blueberries
150g raspberries
500g strawberries, quartered
orange syrup
½ cup (110g) caster sugar
½ cup (125ml) water
1 tablespoon finely grated orange rind
2 tablespoons fresh orange juice, strained

1 Make orange syrup.
2 Beat egg whites in small bowl with electric mixer until soft peaks form. Gradually add a quarter of the hot orange syrup, continue beating until firm peaks form.
3 Place cheese in large bowl; stir until smooth. Fold in egg white mixture.
4 Place berries in large bowl; add remaining orange sugar syrup, stir gently to combine. Serve berries with mascarpone mixture, and sweet biscuits, if desired.
orange syrup stir sugar and the water in small saucepan over low heat until sugar is dissolved. Bring mixture to a boil, then add rind and juice. Reduce heat, simmer, 5 minutes or until reduced to ½ cup (125ml).

on the table in 25 minutes
serves 6

Mango and white chocolate rocky road creams

2 medium mangoes (860g), chopped coarsely
1 cup (280g) thick greek-style yogurt
½ cup (125ml) thickened cream
2 teaspoons caster sugar
250g packet white chocolate rocky road, chopped

1 Blend or process half of the mango until smooth. Transfer to medium bowl, fold in yogurt.
2 Beat cream and sugar in small bowl with electric mixer until firm peaks form; fold into mango mixture.
3 Divide half the chopped mango among four serving glasses. Top with half the cream mixture, then rocky road, remaining cream mixture and mango.

on the table in 15 minutes
serves 4

Raspberries with custard cream

240g raspberries
1 tablespoon orange juice
¼ cup (40g) icing sugar
300ml thickened cream
¾ cup (180ml) prepared vanilla custard
8 savoiardi sponge finger biscuits

1 Combine raspberries, juice and 1 tablespoon of the icing sugar in small bowl; stand 10 minutes.
2 Meanwhile, beat cream, remaining icing sugar and custard in small bowl with electric mixer until soft peaks form.
3 Divide cream mixture evenly among four 1 ½-cup (375ml) serving dishes; top with raspberries, serve with sponge fingers.

on the table in 15 minutes
serves 4

Toffeed apples

4 large apples (800g)
30g butter
2 tablespoons caster sugar
⅓ cup (80ml) maple syrup

1 Thinly slice apples crossways. Remove seeds.
2 Melt butter in large frying pan; cook apples until browned both sides. Add sugar, cook about 5 minutes or until sugar melts and toffee forms around the apple.
3 Add maple syrup; stir until heated through.
4 Serve toffeed apples with ice-cream, if desired.

on the table in 15 minutes
serves 4

Figs, honeycomb and cinnamon ice-cream

6 medium figs (360g)
500g fresh honeycomb
500ml vanilla ice-cream, softened
2 teaspoons ground cinnamon

1 Cut figs in half lengthways; cook on heated oiled barbecue
until browned.
2 Cut honeycomb into 2cm strips.
3 Combine ice-cream and cinnamon in medium bowl.
4 Serve hot figs with ice-cream mixture and honeycomb.

on the table in 20 minutes
serves 4
tip fresh honeycomb is available from health food stores.

Nectarines with almond crumble

4 medium ripe nectarines (680g), halved, seeded
2 tablespoons plain flour
¼ teaspoon ground cinnamon
20g butter
1 tablespoon brown sugar
¼ cups (25g) muesli
1½ tablespoons flaked almonds
½ cup (125ml) dessert wine

1 Preheat oven to 180°C/160°C fan-forced.
2 Place nectarines, cut-side up in pie plate.
3 Combine flour and cinnamon in small bowl; rub in butter with fingertips.
Stir in sugar, muesli and almonds; spoon mixture on top of each
nectarine half.
4 Pour wine into pie plate around base of nectarines; bake 15 minutes or
until nectarines are soft and topping is lightly browned.

on the table in 30 minutes
serves 4

Tropical fruit skewers with coconut dressing

2 medium bananas (400g)
½ medium pineapple (625g)
2 large starfruit (320g)
1 large mango (600g), chopped coarsely
coconut dressing
⅓ cup (80ml) Malibu
¼ cup (60ml) light coconut milk
1 tablespoon grated palm sugar
1cm piece fresh ginger (5g), grated

1 Make coconut dressing.
2 Cut each unpeeled banana into eight pieces. Cut unpeeled pineapple into eight slices; cut slices in half. Cut each starfruit into eight slices.
3 Thread fruit onto skewers, alternating varieties. Cook skewers on heated grill plate (or grill or barbecue), brushing with a little of the dressing, until browned lightly. Serve skewers drizzled with remaining dressing.
coconut dressing place ingredients in screw-top jar; shake well.

on the table in 35 minutes
serves 4
tips you need eight long bamboo skewers for this recipe, soak them in water for about 1 hour before using to avoid them splintering or scorching. We used Malibu for the dressing, but you can use any coconut-flavoured liqueur you prefer.

Waffles with rhubarb berry sauce

400g rhubarb, chopped coarsely
⅓ cup (75g) caster sugar
1 tablespoon Cointreau
200g frozen mixed berries
4 packaged waffles
200ml vanilla ice-cream

1 Combine rhubarb, sugar and liqueur in medium saucepan; cook, covered, stirring occasionally, over medium heat until rhubarb is just tender. Add berries; stir until heated through.
2 Meanwhile, toast waffles following packet directions.
3 Serve waffles with rhubarb berry sauce and ice-cream.

on the table in 20 minutes
serves 4
tip pancakes can also be used in this recipe. Grand Marnier or Triple Sec can be substituted for Cointreau; use orange juice for a non-alcoholic version.

Grilled peaches and nectarines with nougat mascarpone

3 medium peaches (450g)
3 medium nectarines (510g)
2 tablespoons brandy or orange juice
2 tablespoons caster sugar
1 cup (250g) mascarpone cheese
150g almond nougat, chopped
1 tablespoon icing sugar

1 Preheat grill.
2 Halve the fruit; remove seeds. Place the fruit, cut-side up, on large oven tray. Brush with half of the brandy and sprinkle with sugar.
3 Place fruit under grill about 5 minutes or until softened.
4 Meanwhile, combine cheese, nougat, icing sugar and remaining brandy in medium bowl.
5 Serve fruit with nougat mascarpone.

on the table in 20 minutes
serves 4
tips you can use a honeycomb or chocolate bar in place of the nougat in this recipe. Thick cream can be used as a substitute for the mascarpone.

Oranges in cinnamon syrup

¾ cup (165g) caster sugar
¼ cup (60ml) rum
½ cup (125ml) water
1 strip orange peel
1 cinnamon stick
2 whole cloves
2 cardamom pods, bruised
4 large oranges (1.2kg), peeled

1 Stir sugar, rum and the water in medium saucepan over medium heat, without boiling, until sugar is dissolved. Add orange peel and spices, bring to a boil. Simmer, uncovered, about 5 minutes or until thickened slightly.
2 Remove pan from heat, add oranges; stand 5 minutes.
3 Serve oranges and a little syrup with ice-cream, if desired.

on the table in 20 minutes
serves 4

Grilled bananas with mango sorbet

4 small bananas (520g)
2 tablespoons brown sugar
2 medium passionfruit
500mls mango sorbet

1 Preheat grill.
2 Cut unpeeled bananas in half lengthways. Place banana, cut-side up, on oven tray; sprinkle with sugar. Place under grill until sugar is melted and has browned lightly.
3 Serve bananas with sorbet, drizzled with passionfruit pulp.

on the table in 15 minutes
serves 4
tip we used ladyfinger bananas, which are shorter and sweeter than the better-known Cavendish variety. Either type of banana can be used.

DO AHEAD • The following recipes require refrigeration ahead of serving.

Chocolate-dipped fruit

2 medium bananas (400g), sliced thickly
250g strawberries
¾ cup (110g) dried apricots
2½ cups (375g) milk chocolate Melts, melted

1 Line oven tray with baking paper.
2 Dip fruit into chocolate to coat about three-quarters of each piece of fruit; allow excess chocolate to drain away.
3 Place fruit in single layer on tray; refrigerate until set.

• **preparation time** 10 minutes (plus refrigeration time)
  serves 4

Berry trifle

1¾ cups (430ml) thickened cream
¼ cup (40g) icing sugar
1 teaspoon finely grated orange rind
1 cup (250g) mascarpone cheese
¼ cup (60ml) Cointreau
150g blueberries
250g raspberries
250g strawberries, quartered
1 cup (250ml) fresh orange juice
250g savoiardi sponge finger biscuits

1 Beat cream, sugar and rind in small bowl with electric mixer until soft peaks form; fold in cheese and 2 teaspoons of the liqueur.
2 Combine berries and another 2 teaspoons of liqueur in medium bowl.
3 Combine remaining liqueur and juice in another medium bowl. Dip sponge fingers, one at a time, in juice mixture. Arrange half of the sponge fingers around base of 2-litre (8 cup) serving dish. Top with half of the cream mixture; sprinkle with half of the berry mixture.
4 Layer remaining sponge fingers over berries. Repeat cream and berry layers. Cover; refrigerate 3 hours or overnight.

• **preparation time** 20 minutes (plus refrigeration time)
serves 6
tip Grand Marnier or Triple Sec can be substituted for Cointreau.

Fresh mango jellies

1½ cups (375ml) sweet white wine
⅓ cup (75g) caster sugar
3 teaspoons gelatine
½ cup (125ml) water
2 tablespoons lemon juice
2 medium mangoes (860g), sliced thinly

1 Stir wine and sugar in small saucepan over low heat until sugar dissolves; bring to a boil. Reduce heat, simmer, uncovered, 5 minutes.
2 Sprinkle gelatine over the water in small heatproof jug; stand jug in small saucepan of simmering water. Stir until gelatine dissolves.
3 Add gelatine mixture and lemon juice to wine mixture, whisk to combine; cool.
4 Arrange mango in six ¾ cup (180ml) serving glasses. Pour wine mixture over. Cover; refrigerate overnight or until firm.

• **preparation time** 25 minutes (plus refrigeration time)
cooking time 10 minutes
serves 6
tip when dissolved gelatine is added to a mixture, both should be roughly the same temperature.

Tropical fruit salad

2 cups (500ml) water
⅓ cup (135g) grated palm sugar
2cm piece fresh ginger (10g), chopped finely
2 star anise
2 tablespoons lime juice
¼ cup coarsely chopped fresh mint
2 large mangoes (1.2kg), cut into 2cm pieces
1 small honeydew melon (900g), cut into 2cm pieces
1 small pineapple (800g), chopped coarsely
2 medium oranges (480g), segmented
¼ cup (60ml) passionfruit pulp
12 fresh lychees (300g), halved

1 Stir the water and sugar in small saucepan over heat, without boiling, until sugar dissolves; bring to a boil. Boil, uncovered, without stirring, 5 minutes.
2 Add ginger and star anise to pan; simmer, uncovered, further 5 minutes or until syrup thickens slightly. Discard star anise; cool to room temperature. Stir in juice and mint.
3 Place fruit in large bowl with syrup; toss gently to combine. Refrigerate until cold.

• **preparation time** 20 minutes (plus refrigeration time)
cooking time 15 minutes (plus cooling time)
serves 6
tip you need 3 passionfruit for this recipe.

Mango and passionfruit fool

1 large mango (600g), chopped coarsely
1 tablespoon passionfruit pulp
2 egg whites
⅓ cup (75g) caster sugar
400g vanilla yogurt

1 Blend or process mango until smooth. Combine mango puree and passionfruit in small bowl.
2 Beat egg whites in small bowl with electric mixer until soft peaks form. Gradually add sugar, 1 tablespoon at a time, beating until sugar dissolves between additions. Gently fold yogurt into egg white mixture.
3 Layer mango mixture and egg white mixture into four 1½-cup (375ml) serving glasses. Cover; refrigerate 30 minutes before serving.

● **preparation time** 15 minutes (plus refrigeration time)
serves 4
tips frozen mango puree can be used if mangoes are out of season.
You need 1 passionfruit for this recipe.

Individual strawberry royales

250g packet jam rollettes
85g packet vanilla instant pudding mix
2⅓ cups (580ml) cold milk
250g strawberries, chopped finely
300ml thickened cream
2 tablespoons icing sugar
pink food colouring

1 Cut each rollette into quarters; divide rollette quarters among six
1½-cup (375ml) serving glasses, pressing into bases and sides.
2 Sprinkle pudding mix over milk in medium bowl; whisk until combined.
Pour pudding mixture over rollettes; sprinkle with strawberries. Cover;
refrigerate about 30 minutes or until set.
3 Beat cream, sugar and a drop of food colouring in small bowl with
electric mixer until soft peaks form. Spoon equal amounts of cream
mixture over each glass of royale mixture.

• **preparation time** 20 minutes (plus refrigeration time)
serves 6
tip jam rollettes are miniature Swiss rolls.

Fruit salad with star-anise syrup

1 small honeydew melon (900g)
250g strawberries
400g cherries
4 cardamom pods
4 star anise
½ cup (110g) caster sugar
¼ cup (60ml) lemon juice
¼ cup (60ml) water

1 Halve, peel and chop melon coarsely. Hull strawberries; cut in half.
Seed cherries. Place fruit in large bowl.
2 Bruise cardamom pods; place in small saucepan with star anise, sugar,
juice and the water. Stir over heat, without boiling, until sugar dissolves.
3 Pour warm syrup over fruit. Cover; refrigerate about 1 hour or until cold.
Serve with double cream, if desired.

● **preparation time** 30 minutes (plus refrigeration time)
cooking time 5 minutes
serves 4

Strawberries romanoff

500g strawberries, quartered
¼ cup (60ml) orange juice
2 tablespoons icing sugar
2 tablespoons Grand Marnier
300ml thickened cream

1 Combine strawberries, juice, icing sugar and liqueur in medium bowl. Cover; refrigerate 1 hour.
2 Beat cream in small bowl with electric mixer until soft peaks form.
3 Divide half of the strawberry mixture among four ¾-cup (180ml) serving glasses; divide half of the cream among glasses. Repeat layering with remaining strawberries and cream.

● **preparation time** 20 minutes (plus refrigeration time)
serves 4
tip Cointreau or Triple Sec can be substituted for Grand Marnier.

Rhubarb fool

2 cups (250g) coarsely chopped rhubarb
¼ cup (55g) caster sugar
½ cup (125ml) water
½ teaspoon ground cinnamon
¾ cup (180ml) thickened cream
1 tablespoon icing sugar
1 cup (250ml) prepared vanilla custard

1 Combine rhubarb in medium saucepan with caster sugar, the water and cinnamon; bring to a boil. Reduce heat, simmer, uncovered, stirring occasionally, about 10 minutes or until rhubarb is tender. Transfer to large bowl. Cover; refrigerate 1 hour.
2 Beat cream and icing sugar in small bowl with electric mixer until soft peaks form. Stir custard into rhubarb mixture; fold whipped cream mixture into rhubarb mixture.
3 Divide fool mixture among four ⅔-cup (160ml) serving glasses. Cover; refrigerate 1 hour before serving.

• **preparation time** 20 minutes (plus refrigeration time)
cooking time 10 minutes
serves 4
tip you need about 4 trimmed stalks of rhubarb for this recipe.

Mango and raspberry jelly

425g can sliced mango
85g packet mango jelly crystals
2 cups (500ml) boiling water
150g raspberries
85g packet raspberry jelly crystals
1 cup (250ml) cold water
300ml thickened cream

1 Drain mango in sieve over small bowl; reserve liquid. Measure ¼ cup mango slices and reserve. Divide remaining mango slices among eight ¾-cup (180ml) serving glasses.
2 Combine mango jelly crystals with 1 cup of the boiling water in small bowl, stirring until jelly dissolves; stir in reserved mango liquid. Divide evenly among glasses over mango. Cover; refrigerate about 2 hours or until jelly sets.
3 Divide raspberries among glasses over jelly. Combine raspberry jelly crystals and remaining cup of the boiling water in small bowl, stirring until jelly dissolves; stir in the cold water. Divide evenly among glasses over raspberries. Cover; refrigerate about 2 hours or until jelly sets.
4 Beat cream in small bowl with electric mixer until soft peaks form. Using rubber spatula, spread equally among glasses; top with reserved mango.

• **preparation time** 20 minutes (plus refrigeration time)
serves 8
tips if mangoes are in season, you can use one large fresh mango weighing about 600g for this recipe. Peel the mango over a small bowl to catch as much of the juice as possible, then cut off mango cheeks; slice cheeks thinly. Squeeze as much juice as possible from around the mango seed into bowl with other juice; add enough cold water to make 1 cup of liquid to be added to the mango jelly crystals (see step 2).

Tropical fruit salad with lime syrup

⅓ cup (80ml) lime juice
½ cup (125ml) water
½ cup (110g) caster sugar
1 tablespoon green ginger wine
½ small rockmelon (800g)
½ small honeydew melon (800g)
¼ small watermelon (1kg)
½ medium pineapple (600g)
1 small red papaya (650g)
8 lychees or rambutans
2 large or 4 small passionfruit

1 Stir juice, the water and sugar in small saucepan over heat until sugar dissolves; bring to a boil. Simmer, uncovered, 5 minutes. Stir in wine; cool.
2 Meanwhile, chop rockmelon, honeydew melon and watermelon coarsely. Slice pineapple and red papaya thinly. Peel lychees.
3 Combine fruit with passionfruit in large bowl, pour over the syrup; toss gently to combine. Cover; refrigerate 2 hours before serving.

• **preparation time** 15 minutes (plus refrigeration time)
cooking time 10 minutes (plus cooling time)
serves 8
tip lime syrup can be made 3 days ahead; refrigerate.

Stone-fruit jelly

½ cup (110g) caster sugar
3 cups (750ml) sparkling white wine
2 tablespoons gelatine
½ cup (125ml) water
2 tablespoons lemon juice
1 medium nectarine (170g), sliced thinly
2 medium apricots (100g), sliced thinly
1 medium peach (150g), sliced thinly
150g raspberries

1 Combine sugar and 1 cup of the wine in small saucepan; bring to
a boil. Reduce heat, simmer, uncovered, 5 minutes. Transfer to large
heatproof bowl.
2 Meanwhile, sprinkle gelatine over the water in small heatproof jug; stand
jug in small saucepan of simmering water. Stir until gelatine dissolves.
3 Whisk gelatine mixture and juice into warm wine mixture. Stir in
remaining wine.
4 Divide fruit among four 1¼-cup (310ml) serving glasses; pour wine
mixture over fruit. Cover; refrigerate about 3 hours or until set.

• **preparation time** 15 minutes (plus refrigeration time)
cooking time 10 minutes
serves 4
tip we used a sparkling white wine with a sweet, fruity flavour for this recipe.

White chocolate strawberries

12 strawberries
100g white chocolate Melts, melted

1 Line oven tray with baking paper.
2 Dip strawberries in chocolate to coat about three-quarters of the strawberry; allow the excess chocolate to drain away.
3 Place strawberries on tray; refrigerate until set.

● **preparation** 5 minutes (plus refrigeration time)
  serves 4

Fresh peaches and dates with orange flower water

½ cup (125ml) water
½ cup (125ml) caster sugar
pinch saffron threads
4 cardamom pods
⅓ cup (80ml) lemon juice
1-2 teaspoons orange flower water
6 large peaches (1.3kg), sliced
12 fresh dates (250g), quartered
1 cup (280g) thick greek-style yogurt

1 Stir the water, sugar, saffron and cardamom in small saucepan over low heat, without boiling, until sugar is dissolved. Bring to a boil. Reduce heat; simmer, uncovered, about 5 minutes or until mixture just thickens. Cool 10 minutes.
2 Stir in lemon juice and orange flower water to taste.
3 Place peaches and dates in large bowl, strain orange flower water syrup over fruit. Cover; refrigerate 2 hours.
4 Serve fruit with yogurt.

● **preparation time** 10 minutes (plus refrigeration time)
cooking time 5 minutes (plus cooling time)
serves 8
tip orange flower water is available from selected supermarkets, gourmet food stores and delicatessens.

Balsamic strawberries with black pepper wafers

750g strawberries, halved
¼ cup (55g) caster sugar
2 tablespoons balsamic vinegar
¼ cup (35g) plain flour
2 tablespoons caster sugar, extra
1 egg white
30g butter, melted
½ teaspoon vanilla extract
½ teaspoon freshly ground black pepper

1 Preheat oven to 180°C/200°C fan-forced. Line oven tray with baking paper.
2 Combine strawberries, sugar and vinegar in medium bowl. Cover; refrigerate 1 hour.
3 Meanwhile, using wooden spoon, beat flour, extra sugar, egg white, butter and extract in small bowl until smooth.
4 Place 1 level teaspoon of the wafer mixture onto tray; using back of spoon, spread mixture into 8cm circle. Repeat with remaining wafer mixture, allowing 2cm between each wafer. Sprinkle each wafer with black pepper; bake, uncovered, about 5 minutes or until browned lightly. Cool 15 minutes.
5 Serve strawberry mixture with wafers.

• **preparation time** 15 minutes (plus refrigeration time)
cooking time 5 minutes
serves 4

pies tarts +pastries

Apple cinnamon tarts

1 large apple (200g)
1 sheet ready-rolled sweet puff pastry
20g butter, melted
1 teaspoon cinnamon sugar
¼ cup (80g) apricot jam, warmed

1 Preheat oven to 220°C/200°C fan-forced. Grease oven tray.
2 Peel, core and halve apple; slice thinly.
3 Cut pastry sheet in half to form 2 rectangles; place pastry on tray. Overlap apple slices down centre of pastry halves. Brush apple with butter and sprinkle with cinnamon sugar.
4 Bake tarts about 15 minutes or until pastry is browned. Brush with jam.

on the table in 25 minutes
serves 4

Blueberry and fillo pastry stacks

4 sheets fillo pastry
cooking-oil spray
125g packaged light cream cheese
½ cup (125ml) light cream
2 teaspoons finely grated orange rind
2 tablespoons icing sugar
blueberry sauce
300g blueberries
¼ cup (55g) caster sugar
2 tablespoons orange juice
1 teaspoon cornflour

1 Preheat oven to 200°C/180°C fan-forced. Grease oven trays.
2 Spray one fillo sheet with oil; layer with another fillo sheet. Halve fillo stack lengthways; cut each half into thirds to form six fillo squares. Repeat process with remaining fillo sheets. Place 12 fillo squares onto trays; spray with oil. Bake, uncovered, about 5 minutes or until browned lightly; cool 10 minutes.
3 Meanwhile, make blueberry sauce.
4 Beat cheese, cream, rind and half of the sugar in small bowl with electric mixer until smooth.
5 Place one fillo square on each serving plate; spoon half of the cheese mixture and half of the blueberry sauce over squares. Repeat layering process, finishing with fillo squares; dust with remaining sifted sugar.
blueberry sauce cook blueberries, sugar and half of the juice in small saucepan, stirring, until sugar dissolves. Stir in blended cornflour and remaining juice; cook, stirring, until mixture boils and thickens slightly. Remove from heat; cool 10 minutes.

on the table in 25 minutes
serves 4

Apple and rhubarb turnovers

2 medium apples (300g)
20g butter
2 cups (220g) coarsely chopped rhubarb
⅓ cup (75g) firmly packed brown sugar
1 tablespoon lemon juice
½ teaspoon ground cinnamon
2 sheets ready-rolled butter puff pastry
1 egg, beaten lightly
1 tablespoon icing sugar

1 Preheat oven to 200°C/180°C fan-forced. Grease oven tray.
2 Peel and core apples; cut into thin wedges. Melt butter in medium frying pan; cook apple, rhubarb, sugar and juice, stirring occasionally, until sugar dissolves and apple starts to caramelise. Stir in cinnamon; spread mixture on tray. Cool 10 minutes.
3 Cut two 14cm rounds from each pastry sheet. Place a quarter of the fruit mixture on each pastry round; brush around edges with egg. Fold pastry over to enclose filling; pinch edges together to seal. Place turnovers on tray; brush with egg.
4 Bake, uncovered, about 15 minutes or until browned lightly.
5 Dust with sifted icing sugar; serve warm with cream or ice-cream, if desired.

on the table in 35 minutes
serves 4

Plum tarts

1 sheet ready-rolled sweet puff pastry
1 egg yolk
1 tablespoon milk
8 small plums (600g), sliced thinly
1 tablespoons caster sugar

1 Preheat oven to 220°C/200°C fan-forced. Line oven tray with baking paper.
2 Cut pastry sheet into quarters and place on tray; brush each square with combined egg yolk and milk.
3 Overlap plum slices on pastry squares, leaving a 2cm border; sprinkle with cinnamon sugar.
4 Bake on lower shelf about 15 minutes or until pastry is browned and crisp.

on the table in 25 minutes
serves 2
tip cooking time for plums will depend on the ripeness of the fruit.

Chocolate butterscotch tartlets

12 frozen tartlet cases
¼ cup (55g) firmly packed brown sugar
20g butter
¼ cup (60ml) cream
150g dark eating chocolate, chopped coarsely
¼ cup (60ml) cream, extra
2 tablespoons coarsely chopped roasted hazelnuts
1 tablespoon cocoa powder

1 Bake tartlet cases according to manufacturer's instructions.
2 Meanwhile, heat sugar, butter and cream in small saucepan, stirring until sugar dissolves. Reduce heat, simmer, uncovered, without stirring, for 2 minutes. Cool 5 minutes. Stir in chocolate and extra cream; refrigerate 10 minutes.
3 Divide mixture among tartlet cases, sprinkle with nuts and sifted cocoa.

on the table in 35 minutes
makes 12

Peach galette

2 medium peaches (300g)
6 sheets fillo pastry
60g butter, melted
3 teaspoons caster sugar
1 tablespoon apricot jam, warmed, sieved

1 Preheat oven to 200°C/180°C fan-forced. Line oven tray with baking paper.
2 Halve peaches, discard seeds; slice peach halves thinly.
3 Place two pastry sheets on board; brush lightly with a third of the butter. Top with two more pastry sheets; brush lightly with half of the remaining butter. Repeat layering with remaining pastry and butter.
4 Fold pastry in half to form a square; cut 22cm-diameter circle from pastry square. Arrange peach slices on pastry circle; sprinkle with sugar.
5 Bake about 20 minutes or until galette browns. Serve warm galette brushed with jam.

on the table in 35 minutes
serves 4
tips cover the pastry with greaseproof paper then a damp towel when you're working with it, to prevent it drying out. Nectarines, apricots, apples, plums and pears are all suitable to use in place of the peaches.

Spiced apple and fillo cups

425g can pie apples
½ teaspoon ground cinnamon
¼ teaspoon ground nutmeg
½ cup (35g) stale breadcrumbs
¾ cup (120g) sultanas
1½ tablespoons caster sugar
4 sheets fillo pastry
30g butter, melted
1 tablespoon icing sugar

1 Preheat oven to 200°C/180°C fan-forced. Grease eight holes of a 12-hole (⅓-cup/80ml) muffin pan.
2 Combine apple, cinnamon, nutmeg, breadcrumbs, sultanas and caster sugar in medium bowl.
3 Place pastry on a board; brush one sheet with a little of the butter, then top with another sheet. Repeat brushing and layering with remaining butter and pastry. Cut pastry stack into quarters vertically, then across the centre horizontally; you will have eight rectangles. Press one pastry rectangle into each of the muffin pan holes.
4 Divide apple mixture evenly among pastry cases; bake about 10 minutes or until pastry is browned lightly. Using spatula, carefully remove fillo cups from pan; cool 5 minutes on wire rack.
5 Serve fillo cups, dusted with sifted icing sugar.

on the table in 30 minutes
serves 4

Rhubarb galette

20g butter, melted
2½ cups (275g) coarsely chopped rhubarb
⅓ cup (75g) firmly packed brown sugar
1 teaspoon finely grated orange rind
1 sheet ready-rolled puff pastry
2 tablespoons almond meal
10g butter, melted, extra

1 Preheat oven to 220°C/200°C fan-forced. Line oven tray with baking paper.
2 Place butter, rhubarb, sugar and rind in medium bowl; toss gently to combine.
3 Cut 24cm round from pastry sheet, place on tray; sprinkle almond meal evenly over pastry. Spread rhubarb mixture over pastry, leaving a 4cm border. Fold 2cm of pastry edge up and around filling; brush edge with extra butter.
4 Bake, uncovered, about 20 minutes or until browned lightly.
5 Serve dusted with sifted icing sugar, if desired.

on the table in 30 minutes
serves 4

Caramelised apple tarts

1 sheet ready-rolled puff pastry
1 egg yolk
1 tablespoon milk
1 tablespoon caster sugar
2 large apples (400g)
60g butter, softened
⅓ cup (75g) firmly packed brown sugar
½ teaspoon ground cinnamon

1 Preheat oven to 220°C/200°C fan-forced. Grease oven tray.
2 Score pastry in crosshatch pattern with sharp knife. Brush pastry with combined yolk and milk; sprinkle with caster sugar. Cut into four squares; place on tray.
3 Cut unpeeled apples crossways in 5mm slices. Place sliced apples, overlapping if necessary, over base of large baking dish; dot with butter, sprinkle with brown sugar and cinnamon.
4 Bake pastry and apple slices, uncovered, about 10 minutes or until pastry is puffed and browned. Remove pastry from oven. Turn apple slices; bake, uncovered, 10 minutes or until soft and browned.
5 Top pastry with apple; drizzle with caramel mixture in baking dish. Serve with frozen vanilla yogurt or ice-cream, if desired.

on the table in 35 minutes
serves 4

Banana tarte tatin

50g butter
⅓ cup (75g) firmly packed brown sugar
¼ cup (60ml) thickened cream
¼ teaspoon ground cinnamon
3 small bananas (390g), sliced thinly
1 sheet ready-rolled puff pastry
1 egg, beaten lightly

1 Preheat oven to 220°C/200°C fan-forced.
2 Stir butter, sugar, cream and cinnamon in small saucepan, over low heat, until sugar dissolves; bring to a boil. Reduce heat, simmer, uncovered, 2 minutes.
3 Pour caramel sauce into 23cm pie dish; top with banana.
4 Cut 24cm round from pastry sheet. Place pastry sheet over banana, ease pastry into side of dish. Brush pastry with egg; bake, uncovered, about 15 minutes or until pastry is browned.
5 Carefully turn tart onto serving plate; serve immediately.

on the table in 30 minutes
serves 6

DO AHEAD • The following recipes require refrigeration or freezing ahead of serving.

Peanut butter and fudge ice-cream pie

300g packet chocolate chip cookies
40g butter, melted
1 tablespoon milk
1 litre vanilla ice-cream
1⅓ cups (375g) crunchy peanut butter
hot fudge sauce
200g dark eating chocolate, chopped coarsely
50g white marshmallows, chopped coarsely
300ml thickened cream

1 Grease 24cm-round loose-based flan tin.
2 Blend or process cookies until mixture resembles coarse breadcrumbs. Add butter and milk; process until combined. Press mixture evenly over base and side of flan tin: refrigerate 10 minutes.
3 Beat softened ice-cream and peanut butter in large bowl with electric mixer until combined. Spoon pie filling into crumb crust. Cover; freeze pie 3 hours or overnight.
4 Make hot fudge sauce.
5 Drizzle slices of pie with hot fudge sauce to serve.
hot fudge sauce stir ingredients in small saucepan over heat, without boiling, until smooth.

• **preparation time** 20 minutes (plus refrigeration and freezing time)
cooking time 10 minutes
serves 10
tips use a good quality ice-cream; various ice-creams differ from manufacturer to manufacturer, depending on the quantities of air and fat incorporated into the mixture. Warm a large knife under hot water, quickly dry it and cut the pie while the knife is still hot. Marshmallows come in a variety of sizes and colours; the largest white type is best for this recipe.

Lemon cheesecake

250g packet plain sweet biscuits
125g butter, melted
250g packet cream cheese, softened
395g can sweetened condensed milk
2 teaspoons finely grated lemon rind
⅓ cup (80ml) lemon juice
1 teaspoon gelatine
1 tablespoon water

1 Line base of 20cm springform tin with foil or baking paper.
2 Blend or process biscuits until mixture resembles fine breadcrumbs.
Add butter; process until combined. Press biscuit mixture evenly over base
and side of springform tin, place on tray; refrigerate about 30 minutes or
until firm.
3 Meanwhile, beat cream cheese in small bowl with electric mixer until
smooth. Beat in condensed milk, rind and juice; beat until smooth.
4 Sprinkle gelatine over the water in small heatproof jug; stand jug
in small saucepan of simmering water. Stir until gelatine dissolves;
cool 5 minutes.
5 Stir gelatine mixture into lemon mixture. Pour mixture into crumb crust;
cover cheesecake; refrigerate about 3 hours or until set.

• **preparation time** 30 minutes (plus refrigeration time)
serves 8
tip when dissolved gelatine is added to a mixture, both should be roughly
the same temperature. This recipe can be made a day ahead; keep,
covered, in refrigerator.

White chocolate and strawberry cheesecake

185g Butternut Snap biscuits
80g butter, melted
3 teaspoons gelatine
2 tablespoons water
500g packaged cream cheese, softened
395g can sweetened condensed milk
300ml thickened cream
150g white eating chocolate, melted
500g large strawberries, halved
¼ cup (80g) strawberry jam, warmed, strained
1 tablespoon lemon juice

1 Line base of 23cm springform tin with foil or baking paper.
2 Blend or process biscuits until mixture resembles fine breadcrumbs. Add butter; process until combined. Press biscuit mixture evenly over base and side of springform tin, place on tray; refrigerate about 30 minutes or until firm.
3 Sprinkle gelatine over the water in small heatproof jug; stand jug in small saucepan of simmering water. Stir until gelatine dissolves. Cool 5 minutes.
4 Meanwhile, beat cheese and condensed milk in medium bowl with electric mixer until smooth. Beat cream in small bowl with electric mixer until soft peaks form.
5 Stir warm gelatine mixture into cheese mixture; fold in cream and chocolate. Pour cheesecake mixture into springform tin, spreading evenly over biscuit base. Cover; refrigerate overnight.
6 Arrange strawberries on top of cheesecake; brush strawberries with combined jam and juice.

• **preparation time** 25 minutes (plus refrigeration time)
cooking time 5 minutes
serves 10
tips when dissolved gelatine is added to a mixture, both should be roughly the same temperature. Butternut Snap biscuits, made from sugar, flour, rolled oats, butter, coconut and golden syrup, are similar to Anzac biscuits, and can be found at your local supermarket.

Cookies and cream cheesecake

250g plain chocolate biscuits
150g butter, melted
2 teaspoons gelatine
¼ cup (60ml) water
1½ cups (360g) packaged cream cheese, softened
300ml thickened cream
1 teaspoon vanilla extract
½ cup (110g) caster sugar
180g white eating chocolate, melted
150g cream-filled chocolate biscuits, quartered
50g dark eating chocolate, melted

1 Line base of 23cm springform tin with foil or baking paper.
2 Blend or process plain biscuits until mixture resembles fine breadcrumbs. Add butter; process until combined. Press biscuit mixture evenly over base and 3cm up side of springform tin, place on tray; refrigerate about 30 minutes or until firm.
3 Meanwhile, sprinkle gelatine over the water in small heatproof jug; stand jug in small saucepan of simmering water. Stir until gelatine dissolves; cool 5 minutes.
4 Beat cheese, cream, extract and sugar in medium bowl with electric mixer until smooth. Stir in gelatine mixture and white chocolate; fold in quartered biscuits. Pour cheesecake mixture over biscuit mixture in tin, cover; refrigerate about 3 hours or until set.
5 Drizzle with dark chocolate to serve.

• **preparation time** 20 minutes (plus refrigeration time)
cooking time 5 minutes
serves 12
tip when dissolved gelatine is added to a mixture, both should be roughly the same temperature. Place the dark chocolate in a small plastic bag with the corner snipped off to help you drizzle the chocolate evenly over the cheesecake.

Sicilian cheesecake

185g plain chocolate biscuits
90g butter, melted
½ cup (125ml) cream, whipped
60g dark eating chocolate, grated coarsely
filling
650g ricotta cheese
1 cup (160g) icing sugar
1 teaspoon vanilla extract
2 tablespoons crème de cacao
2 tablespoons finely chopped mixed peel
60g dark eating chocolate, grated finely

1 Line base of 20cm springform tin with foil or baking paper.
2 Blend or process biscuits until mixture resembles fine breadcrumbs.
Add butter; process until combined. Press biscuit mixture evenly over base
of springform tin, place on tray; refrigerate about 30 minutes or until firm.
3 Meanwhile, make filling.
4 Spoon filling over biscuit base; refrigerate at least 6 hours or overnight.
5 Spread cream over cheesecake, sprinkle with chocolate.
filling beat cheese, sugar, essence and crème de cacao in large bowl with
electric mixer until smooth and fluffy. Add peel and chocolate; mix well.

preparation time 30 minutes (plus refrigeration time)
cooking time 5 minutes
serves 10

Mars bar cheesecake

250g plain chocolate biscuits
150g butter, melted
2 tablespoons brown sugar
20g butter, extra
300ml thickened cream
50g milk chocolate, chopped finely
3 teaspoons gelatine
¼ cup (60ml) water
500g packaged cream cheese, softened
½ cup (110g) caster sugar
3 x 60g Mars Bars, chopped finely

1 Line base of 20cm springform tin with foil or baking paper.
2 Blend or process biscuits until mixture resembles fine breadcrumbs. Add butter; process until combined. Press biscuit mixture evenly over base and side of springform tin, place on tray; refrigerate 30 minutes or until firm.
3 Meanwhile, combine brown sugar, extra butter and 2 tablespoons of the cream in small saucepan; stir over low heat, until sugar dissolves.
4 Combine chocolate and another 2 tablespoons of the cream in another small saucepan; stir over low heat until chocolate melts.
5 Sprinkle gelatine over the water in small heatproof jug; stand jug in small saucepan of simmering water. Stir until gelatine dissolves; cool 5 minutes.
6 Beat cheese and caster sugar in medium bowl with electric mixer until smooth. Beat remaining cream in small bowl with electric mixer until soft peaks form. Stir slightly warm gelatine mixture into cheese mixture with Mars bars; fold in cream.
7 Pour half of the cheese mixture into tin; drizzle half of the butterscotch and chocolate sauces over cheese mixture. Pull skewer backwards and forwards through mixture several times to create marbled effect. Repeat process with remaining cheese mixture and sauces. Cover cheesecake; refrigerate about 3 hours or until set.

- **preparation time** 30 minutes (plus refrigeration time)
  cooking time 5 minutes
  serves 8
  tips when dissolved gelatine is added to a mixture, both should be roughly the same temperature. Because of the long refrigeration time, this recipe is a good one to prepare a day ahead if you're entertaining.

soufflés+
egg dishes

Coconut custards with papaya

½ cup (135g) grated palm sugar
⅓ cup (80ml) water
3 eggs
⅔ cup (160ml) coconut cream
2 tablespoons milk
1 teaspoon vanilla extract
1 large red papaya (580g)
2 teaspoons grated lime rind
1 tablespoon lime juice
1 tablespoon grated palm sugar, extra

1 Place sugar and the water in small saucepan; cook over low heat until sugar is dissolved.
2 Using a balloon whisk, lightly beat eggs, coconut cream and milk until combined, but not frothy. Gradually whisk hot sugar syrup into egg mixture, then stir in extract. Strain custard into heatproof jug.
3 Pour custard into four ⅔-cup (160ml) heatproof dishes. Place dishes in bamboo steamer, cover dishes with a sheet of baking paper. Place lid on steamer; gently steam about 15 minutes or until just set.
4 Meanwhile, peel and seed papaya; cut into quarters. Combine papaya in medium bowl with rind, juice and extra sugar.
5 Cool custards 5 minutes; serve with papaya mixture.

on the table in 35 minutes
serves 4
tips the custards can be made several hours ahead and served cold, if desired. Store, covered, in refrigerator.

Strawberry meringue cream

500g strawberries, halved
1 tablespoon Grand Marnier
300ml thickened cream
2 tablespoons icing sugar
½ cup (140g) yogurt
10 mini pavlova nests (100g), chopped coarsely

1 Combine strawberries and liqueur in medium bowl.
2 Beat cream and sugar in small bowl with electric mixer until soft peaks form. Fold in yogurt.
3 Place half of the strawberry mixture in 1.25-litre (5-cup) serving dish. Top with half of the pavlova and half of the cream mixture. Repeat layering with remaining strawberries, pavlova and cream mixtures.

on the table in 15 minutes
serves 6
tip Cointreau or Triple Sec can be substituted for Grand Marnier.

Hot chocolate soufflés

2 tablespoons caster sugar
200g dark eating chocolate, chopped
50g butter, chopped
3 egg yolks
7 egg whites
¼ cup (55g) caster sugar, extra
sifted cocoa powder or icing sugar, for dusting

1 Preheat oven to 200°C/180°C fan-forced. Grease eight ½-cup (125ml) ovenproof dishes. Sprinkle bases and sides evenly with caster sugar; shake away excess. Place dishes on oven tray.
2 Stir chocolate and butter in large heatproof bowl over saucepan of simmering water until melted. Remove bowl from heat; stir in egg yolks.
3 Beat egg whites in large bowl with electric mixer until soft form; gradually add extra sugar, beating until dissolved between additions.
4 Using large balloon whisk, gently fold one-third of egg white mixture into chocolate mixture; gently fold in remaining egg white mixture.
5 Divide soufflé mixture among dishes; smooth tops level with tops of dishes. Bake, uncovered, about 12 minutes or until soufflés are puffed.
6 Dust soufflés quickly with sifted cocoa powder or icing sugar; serve immediately with vanilla ice-cream, if desired.

on the table in 30 minutes
serves 8
tip the soufflés must be made just before serving.

Pavlova stacks with banana and caramel sauce

1 cup (250ml) cream
8 mini pavlova nests (80g)
2 medium bananas (400g), sliced thinly
caramel sauce
1 cup (220g) caster sugar
½ cup (125ml) water
⅔ cup (160ml) cream

1 Make caramel sauce.
2 Beat cream in small bowl with electric mixer until soft peaks form.
3 Place half the pavlova nests on serving plates. Divide half of the cream among pavlovas, top with half of the banana; drizzle each with a tablespoon of the caramel sauce. Repeat layering with remaining pavlovas, cream, banana and caramel sauce.
caramel sauce stir sugar and the water in medium heavy-based saucepan over heat, without boiling, until sugar dissolves; bring to a boil. Reduce heat, simmer, without stirring, until mixture is golden brown. Remove from heat, whisk in cream; return to heat, simmer 1 minute.

on the table in 20 minutes
serves 4

Grilled sabayon peaches

6 medium peaches (900g), sliced thickly
4 egg yolks
2 tablespoons caster sugar
2 tablespoons peach liqueur
2 tablespoons apple juice

1 Arrange peach slices in six shallow 1-cup (250ml) ovenproof
serving dishes.
2 Place egg yolks, sugar, liqueur and juice in large bowl over saucepan
of simmering water, ensuring that water doesn't touch bottom of bowl.
Whisk constantly about 8 minutes or until mixture is very thick and creamy.
3 Meanwhile, preheat grill.
4 Spoon warm sabayon evenly over peach slices.
5 Place dishes under grill about 1 minute or until just browned lightly.
Serve immediately.

on the table in 25 minutes
serves 6
tip sabayon is a light, foamy custard that has been whisked over
simmering water in order to cook the egg yolks as it thickens.

Hot passionfruit soufflés

1 tablespoon caster sugar
2 egg yolks
½ cup (125ml) passionfruit pulp
1 teaspoon finely grated lemon rind
½ cup (80g) icing sugar, sifted
4 egg whites

1 Preheat oven to 200°C/180°C fan-forced. Grease six ¾-cup (180ml) ovenproof dishes. Sprinkle bases and sides evenly with caster sugar; shake away excess. Place dishes on oven tray.
2 Whisk egg yolks in medium bowl with passionfruit, rind and 2 tablespoons of the icing sugar until combined.
3 Beat egg whites in small bowl with electric mixer until soft peaks form. Add remaining icing sugar; continue beating until firm peaks form. Fold a quarter of the egg white mixture into passionfruit mixture; gently fold in remaining egg white mixture.
4 Spoon into dishes; bake about 10 minutes or until soufflés are well risen and browned.
5 Serve immediately dusted with extra sifted icing sugar, if desired.

on the table in 20 minutes
serves 6
tips you will need 6 passionfruit for this recipe. The soufflés must be made just before serving.

185

Warm lemon meringue pots

2 tablespoons cornflour
½ cup (110g) caster sugar
¼ cup (60ml) lemon juice
½ cup (125ml) water
1 teaspoon finely grated lemon rind
2 eggs, separated
30g butter, chopped
2 tablespoons cream
⅓ cup (75g) caster sugar, extra

1 Preheat oven to 200°C/180°C fan-forced.
2 Blend cornflour and sugar with juice and the water in small saucepan; stir over heat until mixture boils and thickens. Reduce heat, simmer, uncovered, 1 minute. Remove from heat; stir in rind, egg yolks, butter and cream.
3 Divide lemon mixture among four ½-cup (125ml) ovenproof dishes; place dishes on oven tray.
4 Meanwhile, beat egg whites in small bowl with electric mixer until soft peaks form; gradually add extra sugar, 1 tablespoon at a time, beating until sugar dissolves between additions. Spoon meringue evenly over lemon mixture.
5 Bake, uncovered, about 5 minutes or until meringue is browned lightly.

on the table in 25 minutes
serves 4
tip this dessert is best served hot.

Floating islands in cardamom cream

2 egg whites
⅓ cup (75g) caster sugar
⅔ cup (160ml) cream
2 teaspoons honey
½ teaspoon ground cardamom
⅓ cup (60g) coarsely chopped pistachios

1 Preheat oven to 160°C/140°C fan-forced. Grease four ¾-cup (180ml) ovenproof dishes.
2 Beat egg whites in small bowl with electric mixer until soft peaks form; gradually add sugar, 1 tablespoon at a time, beating until sugar dissolves between additions.
3 Divide egg white mixture among dishes; using spatula, smooth tops. Place dishes in large deep baking dish; pour enough boiling water into baking dish to come halfway up sides of dishes.
4 Bake, uncovered, about 12 minutes or until floating islands have risen by about a third. Stand in baking dish 2 minutes.
5 Meanwhile, combine cream, honey and cardamom in small jug.
6 Divide cardamom cream among serving plates; turn floating islands onto cream, sprinkle with nuts.

on the table in 30 minutes
serves 4
tip cardamom cream will intensify in flavour if made a few hours before serving.

Crushed pavlovas with honey yogurt and mixed berries

250g strawberries, halved
150g blueberries
120g raspberries
10 mini pavlova shells (100g)
1kg honey yogurt

1 Combine berries in medium bowl. Crush pavlovas coarsely into small bowl.
2 Divide yogurt among serving bowls; sprinkle with berries and pavlova.

on the table in 15 minutes
serves 6
tips we used mini pavlova shells here, but a single large pavlova shell can be used instead. Use any combination of your favourite berries in this recipe; if fresh ones are unavailable, you can use thawed frozen berries.

Plum and macaroon trifles

¾ cup (180ml) cream
¾ cup (180g) sour cream
1 tablespoon icing sugar
½ teaspoon vanilla extract
125g packet coconut macaroons
2 tablespoons orange juice
8 small plums (600g), chopped coarsely

1 Beat combined creams, icing sugar and extract in small bowl with electric mixer until soft peaks form.
2 Reserve 4 of the macaroons for decoration. Divide half of remaining macaroons among four 1-cup (250ml) serving glasses; sprinkle 1 teaspoon of the orange juice over macaroons in each glass.
3 Top with half the plums, then half of the cream mixture. Repeat layers with remaining macaroons, juice, plums and cream mixture.
4 Decorate tops with crushed reserved macaroons.

on the table in 10 minutes
serves 4

Sour cherry baked custards

1 cup (200g) drained morello cherries
3 eggs
1 teaspoon vanilla extract
½ cup (110g) caster sugar
2 cups (500ml) hot milk
2 teaspoons custard powder
1 tablespoon cold milk
½ teaspoon ground cinnamon

1 Preheat oven to 160°C/140°C fan-forced.
2 Pat dry cherries with absorbent paper; divide among four shallow ¾-cup (180ml) ovenproof dishes.
3 Whisk eggs, extract and sugar in medium bowl; gradually whisk hot milk into egg mixture.
4 Blend custard powder with cold milk in small bowl until smooth; whisk into egg mixture.
5 Pour custard mixture over cherries; bake, uncovered, about 25 minutes or until just set. Serve warm or cooled sprinkled with cinnamon.

on the table in 35 minutes
serves 4
tips sour or morello cherries are available in jars. You can use any canned fruit of your choice.

Zabaglione

2 eggs
4 egg yolks
½ cup (110g) caster sugar
⅓ cup (80ml) marsala
12 savoiardi sponge finger biscuits

1 Place eggs, egg yolks and sugar in large heatproof bowl over saucepan of simmering water, ensuring that water does not touch bottom of bowl.
2 Beat egg mixture constantly with electric mixer or whisk until light and fluffy. Gradually add marsala while continuing to whisk for about 10 minutes or until mixture is thick and creamy.
3 Spoon zabaglione into small serving glasses; serve with sponge finger biscuits.

on the table in 20 minutes
serves 6
tip zabaglione must be made just before serving.

Strawberry yogurt crunch

250g strawberries, chopped coarsely
2 teaspoons caster sugar
½ cup (125ml) thickened cream
¾ cup (210g) thick greek-style yogurt
pulp of 1 passionfruit
4 mini pavlova nests (40g), crumbled coarsely

1 Combine strawberries and sugar in small bowl; stand 20 minutes.
2 Meanwhile, whip cream in small bowl until thick; fold in yogurt and passionfruit, then meringue and strawberry mixture.
3 Spoon mixture into four 1-cup (250ml) serving glasses.

on the table in 30 minutes
serves 4

DO AHEAD • This recipe requires refrigeration ahead of serving.

Crème catalana

8 egg yolks
1 cup (220g) caster sugar
1.125 litres (4½ cups) milk
2 teaspoons finely grated lemon rind
1 cinnamon stick
½ cup (75g) cornflour
⅓ cup (75g) caster sugar, extra

1 Beat yolks and sugar in large bowl with balloon whisk until creamy.
2 Stir 1 litre (4 cups) of the milk, rind and cinnamon in large saucepan over medium heat until mixture just comes to a boil. Remove immediately from heat. Strain milk into large heatproof jug; pour milk into egg mixture, whisking constantly.
3 Blend remaining milk and cornflour in small jug until smooth; stir into egg mixture. Return mixture to pan; stir constantly over heat until mixture boils and thickens.
4 Pour mixture into 26cm heatproof pie dish. Cover; refrigerate 4 hours or overnight.
5 Just before serving, sprinkle with extra sugar. Place under preheated grill until sugar is caramelised.

• **preparation time** 10 minutes
cooking time 10 minutes (plus refrigeration time)
serves 8
tips custard mixture can be made a day ahead. Caramelise the sugar just before serving.

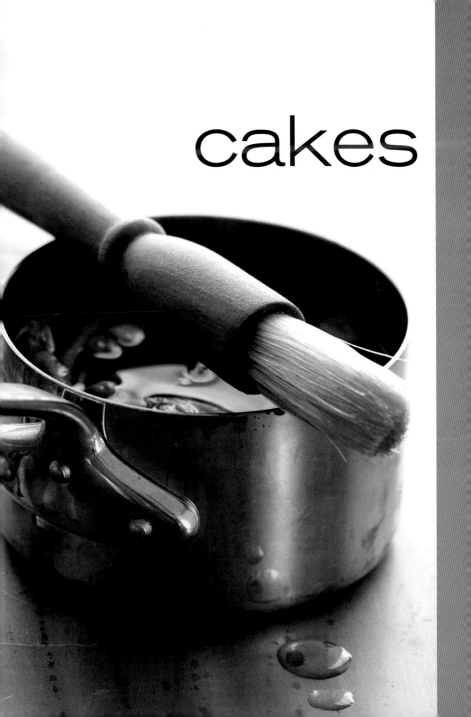

cakes

Little lime syrup cakes

125g butter, chopped
½ cup (110g) caster sugar
2 teaspoons grated lime rind
2 eggs
1 cup (150g) self-raising flour
½ cup (125ml) buttermilk
lime syrup
⅓ cup (80ml) lime juice
½ cup (110g) caster sugar
2 tablespoons water
1 teaspoon grated lime rind

1 Preheat oven to 180°C/160°C fan-forced. Grease six-hole mini fluted tube pan or texas (¾-cup/180ml) muffin pan.
2 Beat butter, sugar and rind in small bowl with electric mixer until light and fluffy. Add eggs, one at a time, beating until just combined between additions.
3 Transfer mixture to medium bowl; stir in sifted flour and buttermilk.
4 Divide mixture among pan holes, smooth tops. Bake, uncovered, about 25 minutes.
5 Meanwhile, make lime syrup.
6 Stand cakes 5 minutes before turning onto wire rack over a tray. Pour hot lime syrup evenly over hot cakes. Serve cakes warm or cooled with whipped cream, if desired.
lime syrup stir all ingredients except grated lime rind in small saucepan over low heat until sugar dissolved. Bring to a boil; remove from heat. Strain into medium heatproof jug. Stir in grated lime rind.

on the table in 35 minutes
makes 6
tip if buttermilk is unavailable, substitute ½ cup (125ml) reduced-fat milk combined with 2 teaspoons lemon juice.

Lemon cakes with passionfruit syrup

1¼ cups (185g) self-raising flour
¼ cup (55g) caster sugar
2 teaspoons finely grated lemon rind
1 egg, beaten lightly
40g butter, melted
2 tablespoons milk
¾ cup (210g) yogurt
passionfruit syrup
1 cup (250ml) water
¼ cup (55g) caster sugar
1 teaspoon cornflour
½ cup (125ml) passionfruit pulp
2 tablespoons finely sliced lemon rind

1 Preheat oven to 180°C/160°C fan-forced. Grease eight holes of a
12-hole (⅓-cup/80ml) muffin pan.
2 Combine flour, sugar and rind in medium bowl. Add egg, butter, milk and
yogurt; stir until just combined. Divide mixture among muffin pan holes;
bake, uncovered, about 25 minutes.
3 Meanwhile, make passionfruit syrup.
4 Stand cakes in pan 5 minutes; turn out onto wire rack. Serve lemon
cakes with passionfruit syrup.
passionfruit syrup stir the water and sugar in small saucepan over heat
until sugar dissolves; bring to a boil. Reduce heat, simmer, uncovered,
without stirring, 10 minutes. Stir in blended cornflour and passionfruit
until mixture boils and thickens. Strain into small heatproof jug; discard
seeds. Stir in rind; cool 10 minutes.

on the table in 35 minutes
makes 8
tips lime rind can be substituted for lemon rind. You will need about six
passionfruit to make this recipe. The thin-skinned purple-black variety will
yield much more pulp than the thicker-skinned Panama passionfruit.

Chocolate fudge cakes with coffee syrup

½ cup (50g) cocoa powder
1 cup (220g) firmly packed brown sugar
½ cup (125ml) boiling water
85g dark eating chocolate, chopped finely
2 egg yolks
¼ cup (30g) almond meal
⅓ cup (50g) wholemeal plain flour
4 egg whites
coffee syrup
¾ cup (165g) firmly packed brown sugar
¾ cup (180ml) water
1 tablespoon instant coffee powder

1 Preheat oven to 160°C/140°C fan-forced. Grease 12-hole (⅓-cup/80ml) muffin pan.
2 Combine sifted cocoa and sugar in large bowl; blend in the water then chocolate, stir until smooth. Stir in egg yolks, almond meal and flour.
3 Beat egg whites in small bowl with electric mixer until soft peaks form. Fold egg whites into chocolate mixture, in two batches; divide mixture among muffin pan holes. Bake, uncovered, about 20 minutes.
4 Meanwhile, make coffee syrup.
5 Stand cakes in pan 5 minutes, before dividing among serving plates. Drizzle hot cakes with hot coffee syrup.

coffee syrup stir sugar and the water in small saucepan over low heat until sugar dissolves; bring to a boil. Reduce heat, simmer, uncovered, without stirring, about 15 minutes or until syrup thickens. Stir in coffee; strain into small heatproof jug.

on the table in 35 minutes
makes 12

Orange and date dessert muffins

2 cups (300g) self-raising flour
½ cup (75g) plain flour
½ teaspoon bicarbonate of soda
1¼ cups (275g) firmly packed brown sugar
125g butter, melted
1 cup (250ml) buttermilk
1 egg, beaten lightly
2 teaspoons finely grated orange rind
1 cup (140g) coarsely chopped dates
orange sauce
¾ cup (165g) firmly packed brown sugar
2 teaspoons cornflour
⅓ cup (80ml) orange juice
2 tablespoons Grand Marnier
125g butter, chopped
2 tablespoons finely grated orange rind

1 Preheat oven to 200°C/180°C fan-forced. Line 12-hole (⅓-cup/80ml) muffin pan with muffin cases.
2 Sift flours and soda into large bowl. Stir in sugar, then add butter, buttermilk, egg, rind and dates, stirring until just combined. Divide mixture among muffin cases.
3 Bake, uncovered, about 20 minutes. Stand 5 minutes.
4 Meanwhile, make orange sauce.
5 Serve muffins warm with orange sauce.
orange sauce combine sugar and cornflour in small saucepan, gradually stir in juice and liqueur; bring to a boil, stirring, until sauce boils and thickens. Add butter and rind; stir until butter dissolves.

on the table in 30 minutes
makes 12
tip Cointreau or Triple Sec can be substituted for Grand Marnier.

Orange almond cakes with cardamom syrup

80g butter, softened
2 teaspoons finely grated orange rind
½ cup (110g) caster sugar
3 eggs
1½ cups (185g) almond meal
⅓ cup (50g) rice flour
⅓ cup (25g) flaked almonds, chopped finely
cardamom syrup
1 medium orange (240g)
½ cup (110g) caster sugar
½ cup (125ml) water
6 cardamom pods, bruised

1 Preheat oven to 180°C/160°C fan-forced. Grease six ½-cup (125ml) oval or rectangular friand pans; place on oven tray.
2 Beat butter, rind and sugar in small bowl with electric mixer until light and fluffy. Beat in eggs, one at a time, beating until combined between additions. Mixture may curdle at this stage but will come together later. Stir in almond meal, flour and almonds.
3 Divide mixture among pans; bake, uncovered, about 20 minutes.
4 Meanwhile, make cardamom syrup.
5 Stand cakes 5 minutes. Turn onto wire rack over tray; turn top-side up, pour hot syrup over hot cakes.
cardamom syrup using vegetable peeler, remove rind from orange; shred rind finely. Juice the orange; place ⅓ cup (80ml) of juice in small saucepan with shredded rind, sugar, the water and cardamom. Stir over heat, without boiling, until sugar dissolves; bring to a boil. Boil, uncovered, without stirring, about 10 minutes or until mixture thickens slightly; discard cardamom, transfer syrup to small heatproof jug.

on the table in 35 minutes
makes 6

Mini lemon yogurt cakes with syrup

⅓ cup (50g) self-raising flour
¼ cup (55g) caster sugar
1½ tablespoons cornflour
¼ teaspoon bicarbonate of soda
1 teaspoon poppy seeds
1 egg yolk
¼ cup (70g) yogurt
½ teaspoon finely grated lemon rind
1 teaspoon lemon juice
10g butter, melted
lemon syrup
1 medium lemon (140g)
¼ cup (55g) caster sugar
¼ cup (60ml) water

1 Preheat oven to 180°C/160°C fan-forced.
2 Sift flour, sugar, cornflour and soda into small bowl; stir in seeds, yolk, yogurt, rind, juice and butter.
3 Drop rounded teaspoons of mixture into baby patty cases on oven tray.
4 Bake, uncovered, about 10 minutes.
5 Meanwhile, make lemon syrup.
6 Drizzle or brush hot lemon syrup over hot cakes.

lemon syrup using vegetable peeler, remove rind from lemon; shred peel finely. Juice the peeled lemon; place 2 teaspoons of the juice (reserve remainder for another use) in small saucepan with shredded rind, sugar and the water. Stir over heat, without boiling, until sugar dissolves. Boil, uncovered, without stirring, about 5 minutes or until mixture thickens slightly; transfer to small heatproof jug.

on the table in 25 minutes
makes 30

Choc-brownies with caramel sauce

80g butter
150g dark eating chocolate, chopped coarsely
¾ cup (165g) firmly packed brown sugar
2 eggs, beaten lightly
1 teaspoon vanilla extract
¾ cup (110g) plain flour
300ml vanilla ice-cream
⅓ cup (50g) vienna almonds, chopped coarsely
caramel sauce
⅔ cup (160ml) cream
60g butter
¾ cup (150g) firmly packed brown sugar

1 Preheat oven to 220°C/200°C fan-forced. Grease six-hole texas (¾-cup/180ml) muffin pan.
2 Combine butter, chocolate and sugar in medium saucepan; stir over medium heat until smooth. Stir in egg, extract and flour.
3 Divide mixture among muffin pan holes, cover pan tightly with foil. Bake about 20 minutes. Remove foil; stand 5 minutes.
4 Meanwhile, make caramel sauce.
5 Place brownies on serving plates; top with ice-cream, caramel sauce and almonds.

caramel sauce stir all ingredients in small saucepan over medium heat until smooth; simmer 2 minutes.

on the table in 30 minutes
serves 6
tip vienna almonds are toffee-coated almonds available from selected supermarkets, nut stands, and speciality confectionery stores.

DO AHEAD • The following recipes require longer preparation ahead of serving.

Moist orange cake

4 large oranges (1.2kg)
60g butter
1 cup (220g) caster sugar
2 eggs
⅓ cup (40g) almond meal
1 cup (160g) wholemeal self-raising flour
2 tablespoons milk

1 Preheat oven to 160°C/140°C fan-forced. Grease shallow 23cm-round cake pan; line with baking paper.
2 Finely grate ½ teaspoon of rind from 1 orange; slice 1 tablespoon of thin strips of rind from same orange. Reserve rinds. Squeeze the peeled orange; reserve ⅔ cup (160ml) juice. Peel remaining 3 oranges; separate into segments. Reserve segments.
3 Beat butter, ⅓ cup of the sugar and the finely grated rind in small bowl with electric mixer until pale and creamy. Add eggs; beat until combined. Add almond meal, flour, 1 tablespoon of the orange juice and milk; stir to combine. Spread mixture into pan. Bake, uncovered, about 20 minutes.
4 Meanwhile, combine remaining juice and remaining sugar in small saucepan over heat, without boiling, until sugar dissolves; bring to a boil. Add reserved rind strips, reduce heat; simmer, uncovered, about 3 minutes or until syrup thickens slightly.
5 Remove cake from oven. Stand 5 minutes; turn onto wire rack. Using skewer, pierce cake several times; brush with ¼ cup of the hot syrup. Serve cake sliced, with reserved orange segments and remaining syrup.

• **preparation time** 15 minutes
cooking time 20 minutes (plus standing time)
serves 12

Chocolate roulade with coffee cream

1 tablespoon caster sugar
200g dark eating chocolate, chopped coarsely
¼ cup (60ml) hot water
1 tablespoon instant coffee powder
4 eggs, separated
½ cup (110g) caster sugar, extra
1 teaspoon hot water, extra
300ml thickened cream
2 tablespoons Tia Maria
1 tablespoon icing sugar

1 Preheat oven to 180°C/160°C fan-forced. Grease 25cm x 30cm swiss roll pan; line base with baking paper. Place a piece of baking paper cut the same size as swiss roll pan on board or bench; sprinkle evenly with caster sugar.
2 Stir chocolate, the water and half of the coffee powder in large heatproof bowl over large saucepan of simmering water until smooth; remove from heat.
3 Beat egg yolks and extra caster sugar in small bowl with electric mixer until thick and creamy; fold egg mixture into warm chocolate mixture.
4 Meanwhile, beat egg whites in small bowl with electric mixer until soft peaks form; fold egg whites, in two batches, into chocolate mixture. Spread into pan; bake, uncovered, about 10 minutes.
5 Turn cake onto sugared paper, peeling baking paper away; use serrated knife to cut away crisp edges from all sides. Cover cake with tea towel; cool.
6 Dissolve remaining coffee powder in the extra water in small bowl. Add cream, liqueur and icing sugar; beat with electric mixer until firm peaks form. Spread cake evenly with cream mixture. Roll cake, from long side, by lifting paper and using it to guide the roll into shape. Cover roll; refrigerate 30 minutes before serving.

• **preparation time** 20 minutes (plus refrigeration time)
cooking time 10 minutes (plus cooling time)
serves 8
tips be sure you beat the egg yolk mixture until thick, and the egg whites only until soft peaks form. Overbeating will dry out the egg whites and make them difficult to fold into the chocolate mixture. Kahlua and crème de cacao can be substituted for Tia Maria.

puddings

Microwave orange and raspberry self-saucing pudding

¼ cup (20g) flaked almonds
30g butter
¾ cup (110g) self-raising flour
⅓ cup (80ml) milk
⅔ cup (150g) firmly packed brown sugar
2 teaspoons finely grated orange rind
¾ cup (110g) frozen raspberries
¼ cup (60ml) orange juice
¾ cup (180ml) boiling water

1 Grease shallow 1.5-litre (6-cup) microwave-safe dish.
2 Place nuts in small microwave-safe bowl; cook, uncovered, in microwave oven on HIGH (100%) about 2 minutes or until browned lightly.
3 Place butter in medium microwave-safe bowl; cook, uncovered, in microwave oven on HIGH (100%) 30 seconds. Add flour, milk and half of the sugar; whisk until smooth. Stir in rind and raspberries; spread into prepared dish.
4 Sprinkle remaining sugar over raspberry mixture; carefully pour over combined juice and boiling water.
5 Place pudding on microwave-safe rack; cook, uncovered, in microwave oven on MEDIUM-HIGH (70%-80%) about 12 minutes. Stand 5 minutes.
6 Sprinkle pudding with nuts. Serve with cream or ice-cream, if desired.

on the table in 25 minutes
serves 4
tip this dish can also be made in a greased 1.5-litre (6-cup) ovenproof dish; bake, uncovered, at 200°C/180°C for about 20 minutes.

Toblerone fondue

200g Toblerone, chopped coarsely
½ cup (125ml) thickened cream
1 tablespoon Kahlua

1 Stir Toblerone and cream in small saucepan until smooth. Remove from heat; stir in liqueur. Transfer fondue to serving bowl.
2 Place fondue in centre of dining table; serve with fresh fruit and biscotti.

on the table in 10 minutes
serves 6
tip Tia Maria can be substituted for Kahlúa.

Chocolate rum mini mousse

6 egg yolks
⅓ cup (75g) caster sugar
½ cup (125ml) dark rum, warmed
50g dark eating chocolate, grated finely

1 Beat egg yolks and sugar in small deep-sided heatproof bowl with electric mixer until light and fluffy.
2 Place bowl over small saucepan of simmering water; whisk egg mixture constantly while gradually adding rum. Continue to whisk until mixture is thick and creamy. Add chocolate, in two batches, whisking gently until chocolate melts between additions.
3 Pour mousse mixture into four ⅓-cup (80ml) serving glasses.

on the table in 15 minutes
serves 4
tips the mousse can be served chilled if desired; refrigerate about 2 hours. A variation on the Italian zabaglione, the rum and chocolate transform this into a dessert of great depth and contrasting flavours. Use a Caribbean rum for this recipe, for its mild, smooth taste.

Butterscotch and white chocolate fondue

1 cup (200g) firmly packed brown sugar
⅓ cup (115g) golden syrup
50g butter
300ml cream
100g white eating chocolate, chopped coarsely

1 Stir sugar, golden syrup, butter and cream in medium saucepan over heat until sugar dissolves and butter melts; bring to a boil. Boil, uncovered, 1 minute. Remove from heat; cool 5 minutes.
2 Add chocolate; stir until smooth. Stand 10 minutes before serving.

on the table in 35 minutes
serves 6
tips the cream mixture must be cooled for 5 minutes before adding chocolate to avoid the chocolate "seizing", that is, becoming grainy and firm and having the appearance of a dull paste. Serve this fondue with the fresh fruit of your choice. We particularly like banana, kiwi fruit, pear, apple and strawberries.

Chocolate hazelnut self-saucing puddings

½ cup (125ml) milk
40g dark cooking chocolate, chopped coarsely
50g butter
⅓ cup (35g) cocoa powder
½ cup (75g) self-raising flour
¼ cup (25g) hazelnut meal
⅓ cup (75g) caster sugar
⅔ cup (150g) firmly packed brown sugar
1 egg, beaten lightly
¾ cup (180ml) water
40g butter, chopped, extra
200ml vanilla ice-cream
chocolate hazelnut sauce
½ cup (125ml) cream
2 tablespoons brown sugar
50g dark cooking chocolate, chopped finely
⅓ cup (110g) chocolate hazelnut spread
1 tablespoon Frangelico

1 Preheat oven to 180°C/160°C fan-forced. Grease four 1-cup (250ml) ovenproof dishes or cups.
2 Place milk, chocolate, butter and half of the cocoa in small saucepan; stir over low heat until smooth.
3 Combine flour, hazelnut meal, caster sugar and half of the brown sugar in medium bowl. Add chocolate mixture and egg; stir until combined. Divide mixture among dishes.
4 Stir the water, extra butter, remaining brown sugar and remaining cocoa in small saucepan over low heat until smooth. Pour hot mixture gently and evenly over puddings; bake, uncovered, about 25 minutes.
5 Meanwhile, make chocolate hazelnut sauce.
6 Serve puddings with ice-cream; pour over sauce.
chocolate hazelnut sauce place cream and sugar in small saucepan, bring to a boil. Remove from heat, add chocolate; stir until smooth. Add spread and liqueur; stir until smooth.

on the table in 35 minutes
serves 4
tip this is best served hot as the pudding will absorb the sauce on standing.

Mocha trifle

1 tablespoon boiling water
2 tablespoons instant coffee powder
2 tablespoons Tia Maria
1 cup (250ml) prepared vanilla custard
100g dark eating chocolate, melted
300ml thickened cream
300g plain chocolate cake
300g raspberries

1 Stir the water, coffee and liqueur in small jug until coffee dissolves.
2 Combine custard and chocolate in small bowl; fold in whipped thickened cream.
3 Halve cake horizontally; trim one half to fit base of deep round 2-litre (8 cup) serving bowl; drizzle with half of the coffee mixture. Sprinkle half of the raspberries over coffee mixture then spread with half of the custard mixture. Repeat with remaining cake, coffee mixture, raspberries and custard mixture. Cover; refrigerate 10 minutes.

on the table in 35 minutes
serves 4
tip it is important the chocolate is cool, but not set, before it is added to the custard. Kahlúa can be substituted for Tia Maria in this recipe.

Apple and brown sugar crumbles

5 medium green apples (750g)
2 tablespoons lemon juice
1 tablespoon brown sugar
¼ teaspoon mixed spice
brown sugar crumble
½ cup (75g) plain flour
80g butter, chopped
⅓ cup (75g) firmly packed brown sugar
¼ teaspoon mixed spice

1 Preheat oven to 200°C/180°C fan-forced. Grease four 1-cup (250ml) ovenproof dishes; place on oven tray.
2 Peel and core apples; chop coarsely. Combine apple, juice, sugar and spice in medium bowl.
3 Make brown sugar crumble.
4 Divide apple mixture among dishes (pile apple high as it shrinks during cooking). Press brown sugar crumble on top of apples.
5 Bake about 25 minutes or until browned.
6 Serve hot with ice-cream or cream, if desired.
brown sugar crumble place flour in medium bowl; rub in butter with fingertips until combined. Add sugar and spice; mix well.

on the table in 35 minutes
serves 4

Buttermilk pancakes with whipped praline butter

2 cups (300g) self-raising flour
⅓ cup (75g) caster sugar
2 eggs, separated
30g butter, melted
1 teaspoon vanilla extract
2 cups (500ml) buttermilk
¾ cup (180ml) maple syrup
whipped praline butter
125g butter, softened
1 tablespoon icing sugar
1 tablespoon maple syrup
⅓ cup (45g) vienna almonds, chopped coarsely

1 Make whipped praline butter.
2 Combine flour and sugar in large bowl; whisk in combined egg yolks, butter, extract and buttermilk.
3 Beat egg whites in small bowl with electric mixer until soft peaks form. Fold a third of the egg white into batter, then fold in remaining egg white.
4 Pour ¼ cup of the batter into large heated oiled frying pan; cook, over medium heat, until browned lightly both sides. Repeat with remaining batter. Serve pancakes with maple syrup and whipped praline butter.
whipped praline butter beat butter in small bowl with electric mixer until pale in colour. Beat in sugar and syrup; fold in nuts.

on the table in 30 minutes
serves 4
tip vienna almonds are toffee-coated almonds available from selected supermarkets, nut stands, and gourmet food and specialty confectionery stores.

Mocha creams

50g dark eating chocolate, chopped coarsely
300ml thickened cream
3 teaspoons instant coffee powder
1 tablespoon warm water
1 egg white
¼ cup (55g) caster sugar
⅓ cup (65g) scorched almonds, chopped coarsely

1 Stir chocolate and ¼ cup of the cream in small saucepan, over low heat, until smooth. Divide mixture among four ¾-cup (180ml) serving glasses; swirl chocolate to coat inside of the glasses. Refrigerate until required.
2 Stir coffee and the warm water in small bowl until coffee dissolves; cool 10 minutes. Beat remaining cream in small bowl with electric mixer until soft peaks form; fold in coffee mixture.
3 Beat egg white in small bowl with electric mixer until soft peaks form. Gradually add sugar, 1 tablespoon at time, beating until sugar dissolves between additions. Fold egg white mixture and ¼ cup of the nuts into cream mixture. Divide mixture among glasses; top with remaining nuts.

on the table in 25 minutes
serves 4

Coconut rice with mango

300ml thickened cream
½ cup (125ml) coconut cream
½ cup (80g) icing sugar
2¼ cups (340g) cooked medium-grain white rice
1 large mango (600g), chopped coarsely
½ cup (25g) toasted flaked coconut

1 Beat cream, coconut cream and sugar in small bowl with electric mixer until soft peaks form.
2 Place rice in large bowl; fold in cream mixture. Cover; refrigerate while preparing mango.
3 Blend or process three-quarters of the mango until smooth; slice remaining mango into thin strips. Divide rice mixture and mango puree, in alternate layers, among four 1-cup (250ml) serving glasses; top with mango strips and coconut.

preparation time 15 minutes
serves 4
tips substitute papaya or berries for mango, if desired. You will need to cook about ¾ cup of medium-grain rice for this recipe.

Apple and berry crumble

800g can pie apple
2 cups (300g) frozen mixed berries
1 tablespoon white sugar
½ cup (125ml) water
1 cup (130g) toasted muesli
2 tablespoons plain flour
1 tablespoon brown sugar
50g butter, chopped
½ cup (20g) cornflakes

1 Preheat oven to 180°C/160°C fan-forced.
2 Combine apple, berries, white sugar and the water in medium saucepan, bring to a boil. Reduce heat, simmer, stirring, until mixture is combined. Remove from heat.
3 Meanwhile, combine muesli, flour and brown sugar in medium bowl; rub in butter with fingertips. Stir in cornflakes.
4 Place apple mixture in 2-litre (8-cup) ovenproof dish; sprinkle with muesli mixture.
5 Bake, uncovered, about 20 minutes or until browned lightly. Serve with custard or ice-cream, if desired.

on the table in 35 minutes
serves 6
tip you can substitute pear for the apple, if you like, or even a single berry variety. Fresh or frozen berries can be used.

Banana caramel puddings

90g butter, melted
½ cup (60g) almond meal
3 egg whites
¾ cup (120g) icing sugar
¼ cup (35g) plain flour
25g butter, melted, extra
2 tablespoons firmly packed brown sugar
2 medium bananas (400g), sliced thickly

1 Preheat oven to 200°C/180°C fan-forced. Grease four 9.5cm-round ⅔ cup (160ml) ovenproof dishes; place on oven tray.
2 Combine butter, almond meal, egg whites, icing sugar and flour in medium bowl; stir until just combined.
3 Divide extra butter among dishes; sprinkle evenly with brown sugar. Divide banana slices then pudding mixture equally among dishes.
4 Bake, uncovered, about 20 minutes or until puddings are browned lightly. Stand puddings 2 minutes before turning onto serving plates.

on the table in 35 minutes
serves 4

Pancakes with choc-hazelnut sauce

1 cup (150g) self-raising flour
1 tablespoon caster sugar
1 cup (250ml) milk
1 teaspoon vanilla extract
1 egg
20g butter, melted
200ml vanilla ice-cream
choc-hazelnut sauce
150g dark eating chocolate, chopped coarsely
⅔ cup (160ml) cream
¼ cup (90g) golden syrup
2 tablespoons hazelnut-flavoured liqueur
20g butter

1 Make choc-hazelnut sauce.
2 Combine flour and sugar in medium bowl; make well in centre.
Gradually whisk in combined milk, extract, egg and butter; strain batter
into large jug.
3 Cook ¼ cups of the batter, in batches, in large heated oiled frying pan
until browned lightly both sides.
4 Top pancakes with ice-cream; drizzle with choc-hazelnut sauce.
choc-hazelnut sauce stir ingredients in small saucepan over heat,
without boiling, until smooth.

on the table in 35 minutes
serves 4

Tiramisu trifle

1 tablespoon instant coffee powder
½ cup (125ml) boiling water
2 tablespoons Sambuca
125g savoiardi sponge finger biscuits
¾ cup (180ml) thickened cream
⅓ cup (55g) icing sugar
2 cups (500g) mascarpone cheese
⅓ cup (80ml) marsala
2 teaspoons cocoa powder

1 Stir coffee and the water in small bowl until coffee dissolves; stir in liqueur. Cut biscuits in half crossways.
2 Beat cream, sugar and cheese in small bowl with electric mixer until soft peaks form; fold in marsala.
3 Dip half of the biscuits in coffee mixture; divide among four 1½-cup (375ml) serving glasses. Divide half of the mascarpone mixture among glasses. Dip remaining biscuits in coffee mixture; divide among glasses, top with remaining mascarpone mixture.
4 Serve dusted with sifted cocoa powder.

on the table in 20 minutes
serves 4
tips Sambuca is an anise-flavoured liqueur. Sherry can be substituted for the marsala, if desired.

Microwave cherry-ripe self-saucing pudding

60g butter, chopped
1½ cups (225g) self-raising flour
1 cup (220g) caster sugar
⅓ cup (35g) cocoa powder
1¼ cups (310ml) milk
1 teaspoon vanilla extract
2 x 55g Cherry Ripe bars, chopped coarsely
½ cup (110g) firmly packed brown sugar
1 tablespoon cocoa powder, extra
2 cups (500ml) boiling water
50g butter, chopped, extra

1 Melt butter in deep 3-litre (12-cup) microwave-safe dish, uncovered, in microwave oven on HIGH (100%) about 1 minute.
2 Add sifted flour, caster sugar and cocoa to dish with milk and extract; whisk until smooth. Stir in Cherry Ripe.
3 Combine brown sugar and sifted extra cocoa in medium jug; gradually stir in the boiling water. Add extra butter; stir until butter melts. Carefully pour syrup mixture evenly over pudding mixture.
4 Cook, uncovered, on HIGH (100%) in microwave oven about 15 minutes or until just cooked in centre. Stand 5 minutes before serving with cream, if desired.

on the table in 25 minutes
serves 8

Minty chocolate mousse

150g dark eating chocolate, melted
4 eggs, separated
2 tablespoons crème de menthe
1 tablespoon caster sugar

1 Combine chocolate, egg yolks and liqueur in large bowl.
2 Beat egg whites and sugar in small bowl with electric mixer until soft peaks form. Fold into chocolate mixture in two batches.
3 Divide mousse mixture among six ¾-cup (180ml) serving glasses; cover, refrigerate about 20 minutes or until set.
4 Serve mousse with fresh raspberries, if desired.

on the table in 35 minutes
serves 6
tip you can replace the crème de menthe with any liqueur of your choice.

Pear and plum amaretti crumble

825g can plums in syrup, drained, halved, stoned
825g can pear halves in natural juice, drained, halved
½ teaspoon ground cardamom
125g amaretti biscuits, crushed
⅓ cup (50g) plain flour
⅓ cup (40g) almond meal
½ cup (70g) slivered almonds
100g butter, chopped

1 Preheat oven to 200°C/180°C fan-forced. Grease 6-cup (1.5 litre) ovenproof dish.
2 Combine plums, pears and cardamom in dish.
3 Combine amaretti, flour, almond meal and nuts in medium bowl. Rub in butter with fingertips; sprinkle evenly over plum mixture.
4 Bake crumble about 15 minutes or until golden brown.

on the table in 25 minutes
serves 4
tip the crumble may also be made in four 1½ cup (375ml) individual dishes; baked for 15 minutes.

Banana pancakes

1 cup (150g) self-raising flour
2 tablespoons caster sugar
1¼ cups (310ml) buttermilk
1 egg, beaten lightly
2 teaspoons maple syrup
20g butter, melted
1 medium banana (200g), sliced thinly
½ cup (60g) pecans, roasted, chopped coarsely
½ cup (125ml) maple syrup, extra

1 Sift flour into large bowl, stir in sugar. Whisk in combined buttermilk, egg, syrup and butter until batter is smooth. Stir in banana.
2 Heat large oiled frying pan. Pour ¼ cup of the batter into pan, allowing room for spreading. Cook until bubbles appear on surface of the pancakes. Turn pancakes; cook until browned. Remove from pan, cover to keep warm. Repeat with remaining batter.
3 Serve pancakes with pecans and extra syrup.

on the table in 20 minutes
serves 4

Marsala and almond mascarpone cheese

1 cup (250g) mascarpone cheese
2 tablespoons marsala
⅓ cup (55g) vienna almonds, chopped coarsely
½ cup (125ml) thickened cream, whipped
1 tablespoon honey
4 savoiardi sponge finger biscuits

1 Combine cheese, marsala, almond, cream and honey in medium bowl.
2 Spoon mascarpone mixture into individual serving glasses. Serve with sponge finger biscuits.

on the table 10 minutes
serves 4

DO AHEAD • The following recipes require refrigeration ahead of serving.

Tiramisu

2 tablespoons ground espresso coffee
1 cup (250ml) boiling water
½ cup (125ml) marsala
250g savoiardi sponge finger biscuits
300ml thickened cream
¼ cup (40g) icing sugar
2 cups (500g) mascarpone cheese
2 tablespoons marsala, extra
50g dark eating chocolate, grated coarsely

1 Combine coffee and the boiling water in coffee plunger; stand 2 minutes before plunging. Combine coffee mixture and marsala in medium heatproof bowl; cool 10 minutes.
2 Place a third of the biscuits, in single layer, over base of deep 2-litre (8-cup) dish; drizzle with a third of the coffee mixture.
3 Beat cream and sugar in small bowl until soft peaks form; transfer to large bowl. Fold in combined cheese and extra marsala.
4 Spread a third of the cream mixture over biscuits in dish. Submerge half of the remaining biscuits, one at a time, in coffee mixture, taking care the biscuits do not become so soggy that they fall apart; place over cream layer. Top biscuit layer with half of the remaining cream mixture. Repeat process with remaining biscuits, coffee mixture and cream mixture; sprinkle with chocolate. Cover; refrigerate 3 hours or overnight.

• **preparation time** 25 minutes (plus refrigeration time)
serves 6
tip savoiardi, from the Piedmont region of Italy, are the traditional sponge-cake-like biscuits used in making a tiramisu, but they're also used in making other semifreddi and charlottes. Be certain the ones you buy are crisp; if soft, they've passed their use-by date.

Black forest parfaits

2 x 85g packets cherry jelly crystals
6 jam rollettes (150g), chopped coarsely
¼ cup (60ml) sweet sherry
425g can stoneless black cherries, drained
1½ cups (375ml) prepared vanilla custard
60g dark eating chocolate bars, sliced

1 Make jelly according to packet instructions; place in large jug.
Refrigerate about 1 hour or until jelly is almost set.
2 Meanwhile, combine rollettes and sherry in small bowl. Reserve half
of the rollette mixture; cover until required. Divide remaining half among
six 1⅓-cup (330ml) serving glasses.
3 Pour half of the jelly mixture evenly over rollette mixture in glasses;
sprinkle with half of the cherries. Refrigerate 5 minutes. Continue
layering with remaining rollette mixture, then all of the custard, the
remaining jelly and, finally, the remaining cherries. Cover parfaits;
refrigerate overnight.
4 Serve parfaits sprinkled evenly with chocolate.

• **preparation time** 30 minutes (plus refrigeration time)
serves 6
tip jam rollettes are miniature Swiss rolls.

Yogurt and mango jelly

85g packet mango jelly crystals
1 cup (250ml) boiling water
2 x 200g cartons five-fruits yogurt
1 medium mango (430g), chopped finely
1 medium banana (200g), sliced thinly
1 medium kiwi fruit (85g), halved, sliced thinly
2 tablespoons passionfruit pulp

1 Stir jelly crystals with the water in small heatproof bowl until dissolved; refrigerate about 20 minutes or until cold (do not allow to set).
2 Add yogurt and mango to jelly; stir to combine. Divide jelly mixture among six 1-cup (250ml) serving glasses. Cover; refrigerate about 2 hours or until set. Just before serving, top each jelly with equal amounts of banana, kiwi fruit and passionfruit.

• **preparation time** 5 minutes (plus refrigeration time)
serves 6
tips we used golden kiwi fruit in this recipe. You need about 2 passionfruit for this recipe.

Berry mousse

2 teaspoons gelatine
2 tablespoons water
2 egg whites
⅓ cup (75g) caster sugar
2 x 200g cartons berry yogurt
150g fresh mixed berries

1 Sprinkle gelatine over the water in small heatproof jug; place jug in small saucepan of simmering water, stir until gelatine dissolves. Cool.
2 Meanwhile, beat egg whites in small bowl with electric mixer until soft peaks form. Gradually add sugar, beating until sugar dissolves.
3 Place yogurt in medium bowl; stir in gelatine mixture, fold in egg white mixture. Spoon mousse mixture into serving bowl, cover; refrigerate about 3 hours or until set. Top mousse with berries to serve.

• **preparation time** 10 minutes (plus refrigeration time)
serves 4
tip when dissolved gelatine is added to a mixture, both should be roughly the same temperature.

Panna cotta

300ml thickened cream
1 cup (250ml) milk
⅓ cup (75g) caster sugar
2 teaspoons vanilla extract
2½ teaspoons gelatine
1 tablespoon water
250g strawberries, halved
¼ cup (60ml) orange juice
2 teaspoons icing sugar

1 Grease six ½-cup (125ml) moulds.
2 Stir cream, milk and sugar in small saucepan over low heat until sugar is dissolved. Stir in extract.
3 Sprinkle gelatine over the water in small heatproof jug. Stand jug in small saucepan of simmering water; stir until gelatine dissolves. Stir into cream mixture.
4 Divide mixture among moulds. Cover; refrigerate about 3 hours or until set.
5 Meanwhile, combine strawberries, juice and icing sugar in medium bowl. Cover; refrigerate 1 hour.
6 Turn panna cotta onto serving plates and serve with strawberry mixture.

• **preparation time** 20 minutes (plus refrigeration time)
cooking time 5 minutes
serves 6
tip panna cotta is a light, silky-smooth "custard". It can be served with seasonal fruit of your choice. When dissolved gelatine is added to a mixture, both should be roughly the same temperature.

Margarita mousse

¼ cup (55g) white sugar
1 tablespoon gelatine
2 tablespoons water
1 cup (220g) caster sugar
1¼ cups (300g) sour cream
300ml thickened cream
½ cup (120g) spreadable cream cheese
green food colouring
¼ cup (60ml) tequila
1 tablespoon Cointreau
1 teaspoon finely grated lime rind
¾ cup (180ml) lime juice
⅓ cup (80ml) orange juice

1 Place white sugar on saucer. Dip rims of six ¾-cup (180ml) serving glasses in bowl of cold water then into white sugar; refrigerate glasses.
2 Sprinkle gelatine over the water in small heatproof jug. Stand jug in small saucepan of simmering water; stir until gelatine dissolves. Cool 5 minutes.
3 Beat caster sugar, sour cream, cream and cream cheese in medium bowl with electric mixer until sugar dissolves and mixture is fluffy. Beat in enough colouring to tint mixture a pale green.
4 Whisk tequila, liqueur, rind, juices and gelatine mixture into cream mixture. Divide mixture among glasses; refrigerate about 3 hours or until mousse sets.

• **preparation time** 20 minutes (plus refrigeration time)
cooking time 5 minutes
serves 6
tips when dissolved gelatine is added to a mixture, both should be roughly the same temperature. Mousse can be prepared a day ahead; refrigerate, covered, until ready to serve.

Cherry cheesecake parfaits

1 tablespoon caster sugar
1 tablespoon kirsch
425g can seeded black cherries, undrained
2 teaspoons cornflour
1 tablespoon water
60g packaged cream cheese
200g french cheesecake yogurt
4 savoiardi sponge finger biscuits, halved

1 Stir sugar, kirsch and cherries in small saucepan over low heat until sugar dissolves; bring to a boil. Remove from heat; reserve ⅔ cup cherry liquid from pan.
2 Return pan to heat, add blended cornflour and the water; cook, stirring, until mixture boils and thickens slightly. Remove from heat; cool 10 minutes.
3 Meanwhile, beat cream cheese with yogurt in small bowl until combined.
4 Dip biscuit halves, one at a time, in reserved cherry liquid. Divide biscuit halves among four ¾-cup (180ml) serving glasses; top each with ⅓ cup of the cherry mixture then a quarter of the cream-cheese mixture. Cover; refrigerate 30 minutes before serving.

● **preparation time** 15 minutes (plus refrigeration time)
cooking time 10 minutes
serves 4

Raspberry and chocolate mousse trifle

150g dark eating chocolate, chopped coarsely
½ cup (125ml) thickened cream
1 egg, separated
2 teaspoons caster sugar
85g packet raspberry jelly crystals
200g packaged chocolate sponge fingers (approximately 6)
¼ cup (60ml) Tia Maria
1 cup (135g) raspberries
300ml thickened cream, extra

1 Combine chocolate and cream in small saucepan; stir over heat, without boiling, until smooth. Remove from heat; whisk in egg yolk. Transfer to medium bowl.
2 Place egg white and sugar in small bowl; beat with electric mixer until sugar dissolves. Gently fold egg white mixture into chocolate mixture. Cover; refrigerate mousse 3 hours or overnight.
3 Meanwhile, make jelly according to manufacturer's instructions; refrigerate until jelly just begins to set.
4 Cut sponge fingers into 1.5cm slices. Place slices over base and around side of deep 2-litre (8 cup) large serving bowl; drizzle evenly with liqueur. Pour jelly over sponge fingers; refrigerate until jelly sets.
5 Sprinkle half of the raspberries over jelly; spread evenly with mousse. Top with whipped extra cream and remaining raspberries. Sprinkle with chocolate shavings, if desired.

- **preparation time** 30 minutes (plus refrigeration time)
  serves 6
  tips if fresh raspberries are not available, frozen raspberries, thawed, can be substituted. In step 3, jelly should set to the same consistency as an unbeaten egg white. Small cakes filled with mock cream are available in 200g packages at most supermarkets. Kahlúa and crème de cacao can be substituted for Tia Maria.

Passionfruit panna cotta with mango

1 cup (250ml) milk
300ml thickened cream
½ vanilla bean, halved lengthways
⅓ cup (75g) caster sugar
⅓ cup (80ml) sieved passionfruit juice
2 teaspoons gelatine
2 tablespoons water
2 small mangoes (600g)
2 passionfruit, extra

1 Grease six ½-cup (125ml) non-metallic moulds.
2 Combine milk, cream, vanilla bean, and sugar in medium saucepan over low heat, until warm. Strain cream mixture into medium jug, discard bean, stir in juice; cool.
3 Sprinkle gelatine over the water in small heatproof jug. Stand jug in small saucepan of simmering water; stir until gelatine dissolves. Stir into cream mixture.
4 Divide mixture among moulds. Cover; refrigerate about 3 hours or until set.
5 Cut mango cheeks from seed, peel; slice mango thinly. Arrange mango on serving plates. Invert panna cotta onto mango; drizzle with extra passionfruit.

• **preparation time** 15 minutes (plus refrigeration time)
cooking time 5 minutes
serves 6
tips you will need about 10 passionfruit for this recipe, which can be made a day ahead. When dissolved gelatine is added to a mixture, both should be roughly the same temperature.

Chocolate nut bavarois with raspberry sauce

1 cup (250ml) milk
½ cup (165g) chocolate hazelnut spread
4 egg yolks
¼ cup (55g) caster sugar
2 teaspoons gelatine
1 tablespoon water
300ml thickened cream
raspberry sauce
200g raspberries
2 tablespoons icing sugar

1 Combine milk and chocolate spread in small saucepan. Stir over heat until chocolate spread melts; bring to a boil. Transfer to medium bowl.
2 Beat egg yolks and caster sugar in small bowl with electric mixer until thick and creamy; gradually stir into chocolate mixture.
3 Sprinkle gelatine over the water in small heatproof jug; stand in small saucepan of simmering water, stirring, until gelatine dissolves. Stir gelatine mixture into warm milk mixture; cool to room temperature.
4 Beat cream in small bowl with electric mixer until soft peaks form; fold into chocolate mixture. Divide bavarois mixture among six ¾-cup (180ml) serving glasses; refrigerate about 3 hours. Top with raspberry sauce.
raspberry sauce push raspberries through sieve into small bowl; discard seeds. Stir in sugar.

• **preparation time** 30 minutes (plus refrigeration time)
cooking time 5 minutes
serves 6
tips if fresh raspberries are not available, you can use frozen raspberries, thawed, instead. When dissolved gelatine is added to a mixture, both should be roughly the same temperature.

Honey and yogurt muscatels

500g thick greek-style yogurt
½ cup (175g) honey
¾ cup (180ml) cream
1 vanilla bean, halved lengthways (or 1 teaspoon vanilla bean paste)
1 teaspoon gelatine
1 tablespoon water
2 egg whites
2 tablespoons caster sugar
honey muscatels
½ cup (125ml) water
¼ cup (90g) honey
50g muscatels

1 Place yogurt in a sieve lined with muslin; place sieve over bowl. Cover; refrigerate overnight.
2 Stir honey, cream and vanilla bean in medium saucepan over low heat until honey is dissolved. Remove from heat.
3 Meanwhile, sprinkle gelatine over the water in small heatproof jug; stand in small saucepan of simmering water, stirring, until gelatine dissolves. Stir gelatine into honey mixture, cool until lukewarm; remove vanilla bean. Stir yogurt into honey mixture until combined.
4 Beat egg whites until firm peaks form, add sugar, beat until dissolved. Fold egg whites into honey and yogurt mixture; pour mixture into six ¾-cup (180ml) serving glasses; cover, refrigerate for about 3 hours or until set.
5 Make honey muscatels.
6 Serve mousse topped with muscatels, drizzled with syrup.
honey muscatels place water, honey, and muscatels in small saucepan; bring to a boil. Simmer, uncovered, about 5 minutes or until syrup has thickened. Cool.

• **preparation time** 10 minutes (plus refrigeration time)
cooking time 5 minutes (plus cooling time)
serves 6
tips when dissolved gelatine is added to a mixture, both should be roughly the same temperature. The flavour of this mousse will be influenced by the type of honey used. Muscatels are large dried grapes on the stem, available from gourmet food stores and some health food stores.

White-choc panna cotta with passionfruit sauce

300ml thickened cream
¾ cup (180ml) milk
150g white eating chocolate, chopped coarsely
⅓ cup (75g) caster sugar
2 teaspoons gelatine
1 tablespoon water
½ cup (125ml) passionfruit pulp
1 cup (250ml) Sauternes-style dessert wine

1 Grease six ½-cup (125ml) moulds.
2 Stir cream, milk, chocolate and 2 tablespoons of the sugar in small saucepan; stir over heat, without boiling, until smooth.
3 Sprinkle gelatine over the water in small heatproof jug. Stand jug in small saucepan of simmering water; stir until gelatine dissolves. Stir into cream mixture.
4 Divide mixture among moulds. Cover; refrigerate about 3 hours or until set.
5 Meanwhile, combine passionfruit, wine and remaining sugar in small saucepan, bring to a boil. Reduce heat, simmer, uncovered, without stirring, about 10 minutes or until passionfruit syrup reduces by a third. Cool.
6 Turn panna cotta onto serving plates; drizzle with passionfruit sauce.

● **preparation time** 20 minutes (plus refrigeration time)
cooking time 10 minutes
serves 6
tips you will need about 6 passionfruit for this recipe. When dissolved gelatine is added to a mixture, both should be roughly the same temperature. Panna cotta can be made a day ahead. Cover; refrigerate overnight. Serve the remaining dessert wine with the panna cotta.

White chocolate and honeycomb mousse

2 eggs, separated
250g white eating chocolate, chopped coarsely
1 tablespoon caster sugar
1 teaspoon gelatine
⅓ cup (80ml) milk
300ml thickened cream
2 x Violet Crumble bars, chopped coarsely

1 Place egg yolks, chocolate, sugar, gelatine and milk in small heavy-based saucepan; stir continuously, over low heat, until mixture is smooth. Transfer mixture to large bowl; cool.
2 Beat egg whites in small bowl with electric mixer until soft peaks form.
3 Beat cream, in separate small bowl, with electric mixer until soft peaks form.
4 Fold cream and honeycomb into chocolate mixture; fold in egg whites. Divide mixture among four 1-cup (250ml) serving glasses. Cover; refrigerate 3 hours before serving.

● **preparation time** 10 minutes (plus cooling and refrigeration time)
cooking time 5 minutes
serves 4
tip care must be taken when heating the white chocolate mixture; if the heat is too high, the chocolate will "seize", that is, it will become clumpy, grainy and, therefore, unusable.

Passionfruit buttermilk puddings

3 cups (750ml buttermilk
½ cup (110g) caster sugar
½ teaspoon vanilla bean paste
3 teaspoons gelatine
1 tablespoon water
6 passionfruit, approximately
¼ small (250g) rockmelon
¼ small (250g) honeydew melon
¼ small (250g) pineapple
1 passionfruit, extra

1 Grease six ⅔-cup (160ml) non-metallic moulds.
2 Stir buttermilk, sugar and vanilla in medium saucepan over low heat until sugar dissolves. Remove pan from heat.
3 Meanwhile, sprinkle gelatine over water in small heatproof jug; place jug in small saucepan of simmering water, stir until gelatine dissolves. Cool slightly.
4 Stir gelatine mixture into buttermilk mixture. Strain through a fine sieve into a jug; cool to room temperature.
5 Scoop pulp from passionfruit. Press pulp in a sieve over a bowl – you need ⅓ cup (80ml) passionfruit juice. Stir juice into buttermilk mixture; pour into moulds. Cover; refrigerate 6 hours or overnight until firm.
6 Slice melons and pineapple; remove pulp from extra passionfruit.
7 Turn moulds onto serving plate, serve puddings with fruit.

• **preparation time** 20 minutes (plus refrigeration time)
cooking time 5 minutes
serves 6
tip when dissolved gelatine is added to a mixture, both should be roughly the same temperature.

Silky chocolate mousse

300g dark eating chocolate, chopped coarsely
50g unsalted butter
3 eggs, separated
1 tablespoon irish cream liqueur
¼ cup (55g) caster sugar
300ml thickened cream, whipped

1 Combine chocolate and butter in small saucepan; stir over low heat until smooth. Remove from heat.
2 Stir in egg yolks, one at a time, then liqueur; transfer mixture to large bowl. Cool.
3 Beat egg whites in small bowl with electric mixer until soft peaks form. Gradually add sugar, 1 tablespoon at a time, beating until sugar dissolves between additions.
4 Meanwhile, fold cream into chocolate mixture, then fold in egg white mixture, in two batches. Divide chocolate mousse among eight ½-cup (125ml) serving dishes. Cover; refrigerate 2 hours or until set.

• **preparation time** 15 minutes (plus refrigeration time)
cooking time 5 minutes
serves 8
tip we used Bailey's Irish Cream in this recipe, but you can use any irish cream liqueur.

ice-creams
+sorbets

Grilled cinnamon doughnuts with maple syrup

6 cinnamon doughnuts
½ cup (125ml) maple syrup
500ml vanilla ice-cream

1 Split doughnuts in half horizontally. Cook doughnuts, in batches, on heated, oiled grill plate until browned lightly both sides.
2 Drizzle doughnuts with maple syrup; serve with ice-cream.

on the table in 10 minutes
serves 4

Ice-cream with fudge sauce

½ cup (125ml) cream
200g dark eating chocolate, chopped
20g butter
¼ teaspoon vanilla extract
1 litre vanilla ice-cream

1 Stir cream, chocolate and butter in small saucepan over low heat until chocolate is melted and sauce is smooth. Stir in extract.
2 Serve warm fudge sauce over ice-cream.

on the table in 15 minutes
serves 4
tip sauce will keep under refrigeration, covered, for up to three days. To serve, reheat sauce briefly in microwave oven on HIGH (100%) or over low heat in small saucepan until it reaches the desired consistency.

Summer berry sundae

¼ cup (55g) caster sugar
500g mixed frozen berries
1 tablespoon Grand Marnier
1 litre vanilla ice-cream
⅔ cup (100g) roasted macadamias, chopped coarsely

1 Stir sugar and berries in medium saucepan over heat, without boiling, until sugar dissolves; bring to a boil. Reduce heat, simmer, uncovered, about 5 minutes or until berries soften. Stir in liqueur; cool 10 minutes.
2 Layer ice-cream, berry mixture and nuts in four serving glasses.

on the table in 20 minutes
serves 4
tip Cointreau or Triple Sec can be substituted for Grand Marnier, or you can use orange juice instead of the liqueur for a non-alcoholic dessert.

Waffles with ice-cream and chocolate peanut sauce

½ cup (125ml) cream
2 x 60g Snickers bars, chopped coarsely
4 belgian-style waffles
300ml vanilla ice-cream

1 Heat cream in small saucepan, add Snickers; stir until melted.
2 Warm waffles according to manufacturer's instructions.
3 Divide waffles among serving plates; top with ice-cream and chocolate peanut sauce.

on the table in 15 minutes
serves 4

Coconut and vanilla parfait

⅓ cup (80ml) coconut cream
1.5 litres vanilla ice-cream, softened
2 tablespoons passionfruit pulp
⅓ cup (15g) flaked coconut, toasted

1 Combine coconut cream and ice-cream in large bowl. Divide mixture evenly between four parfait glasses.
2 Top each parfait with passionfruit pulp and coconut.

on the table in 10 minutes
serves 4

Layered banana split with caramel sauce

⅔ cup (160ml) thickened cream
60g butter
¾ cup (165g) firmly packed brown sugar
1 cup (250ml) thickened cream, extra
2 large bananas (460g), sliced thinly
500ml vanilla ice-cream
½ cup (40g) flaked almonds, toasted

1 Stir cream, butter and sugar in small saucepan, over medium heat, until smooth. Reduce heat, simmer, uncovered, 2 minutes. Cool 10 minutes.
2 Meanwhile, beat extra cream in small bowl with electric mixer until soft peaks form.
3 Divide half of the sauce among four serving dishes; top with banana, cream and ice-cream then remaining sauce and nuts.

on the table in 20 minutes
serves 4

Ice-cream timbales with rocky road sauce

1 litre vanilla ice-cream, softened
2 x 60g Snickers bars, chopped finely
2 x 50g Crunchie bars, chopped finely
⅔ cup (160ml) thickened cream
100g dark eating chocolate, chopped coarsely
100g rocky road, chopped coarsely

1 Line four 1-cup (250ml) metal moulds with plastic wrap.
2 Place ice-cream in large bowl; fold in chocolate bars. Divide mixture among moulds. Cover with foil; freeze about 15 minutes or until firm.
3 Meanwhile, heat cream and chocolate in small saucepan over low heat, stirring until smooth. Remove pan from heat; stir rocky road into sauce mixture.
4 Turn ice-cream timbales onto serving plates; drizzle with rocky road sauce.

on the table in 30 minutes
serves 4

Waffles and ice-cream à la suzette

8 belgian-style waffles
200ml vanilla ice-cream
suzette sauce
125g butter
½ cup (110g) caster sugar
2 teaspoons finely grated orange rind
1 tablespoon orange juice
¼ cup (60ml) Cointreau

1 Make suzette sauce.
2 Warm waffles according to manufacturer's instructions.
3 Divide half of the waffles among serving plates; top with ice-cream, remaining waffles and suzette sauce.
suzette sauce melt butter in small heavy-based saucepan, add sugar, rind, juice and liqueur; cook, stirring, over low heat, without boiling, until sugar dissolves. Bring to a boil. Reduce heat, simmer, without stirring, about 1 minute or until sauce thickens slightly.

on the table in 20 minutes
serves 4
tip Grand Marnier can be substituted for Cointreau.

Ice-cream sundae with berry sauce and almond wafers

⅓ cup (75g) firmly packed brown sugar
25g butter
½ cup (125ml) thickened cream
1 cup (150g) frozen mixed berries
500ml vanilla ice-cream
500ml strawberry ice-cream
almond wafers
1 egg white
2 tablespoons caster sugar
2 tablespoons plain flour
20g butter, melted
2 tablespoons flaked almonds

1 Preheat oven to 180°C/160°C fan-forced. Grease two oven trays.
2 Make almond wafers.
3 Combine sugar, butter and cream in small saucepan; bring to a boil.
Reduce heat, simmer, stirring, about 5 minutes or until slightly thickened.
Remove from heat; stir in berries.
4 Divide both ice-creams among four 1½-cup (375ml) serving glasses;
drizzle with berry sauce. Serve with almond wafers.
almond wafers beat egg white in small bowl with electric mixer until
soft peaks form. Gradually add sugar, beating until dissolved after each
addition; fold in flour and butter. Drop rounded teaspoons of mixture
10cm apart onto trays (approximately four per tray); sprinkle with nuts.
Bake about 5 minutes or until wafers are browned lightly; cool on trays.

on the table in 35 minutes
serves 4

Ice-cream with choc-peanut sauce

2 x 60g Snickers chocolate bars, chopped coarsely
½ cup (125ml) cream
2 tablespoons Tia Maria
1 litre vanilla ice-cream

1 Stir Snickers and cream in small saucepan, without boiling, until Snickers melt and sauce thickens slightly. Remove from heat.
2 Stir in liqueur; stand 5 minutes before serving drizzled over scoops of ice-cream.

on the table in 20 minutes
serves 4
tip Kahlúa can be substituted for Tia Maria.

Lemon meringue sundae

⅔ cup (220g) lemon butter
⅓ cup (80ml) cream
1 litre vanilla ice-cream
4 mini pavlova shells (40g), chopped coarsely

1 Stir lemon butter and cream in small saucepan, over low heat, until smooth; cool 10 minutes.
2 Layer ice-cream, lemon butter mixture and pavlova in four serving glasses.

on the table in 20 minutes
serves 4
tip if you cannot find mini pavlova shells you could use part of whole meringue shell or coconut macaroons.

Pistachio praline with ice-cream

¼ cup (55g) white sugar
1 tablespoon roasted chopped pistachios
1 litre vanilla ice-cream

1 Preheat oven to 220°C/200°C fan-forced. Line oven tray with baking paper.
2 Sprinkle sugar evenly over tray; bake about 8 minutes or until sugar just becomes a light golden-brown toffee. Sprinkle nuts over hot toffee; cool.
3 Break praline into pieces, then process until chopped finely. Serve praline sprinkled over vanilla ice-cream.

on the table in 30 minutes
serves 4

Chocolate sundaes

2 litres vanilla ice-cream
100g marshmallows
½ cup (70g) crushed nuts
12 ice-cream wafers
hot chocolate sauce
200g dark eating chocolate, chopped coarsely
½ cup (125ml) thickened cream

1 Make hot chocolate sauce.
2 Place a little of the hot chocolate sauce in the bottom of six ¾-cup (180ml) serving glasses; top with ice-cream, marshmallows, more chocolate sauce, nuts and wafer biscuits.
hot chocolate sauce stir chocolate and cream in small saucepan over low heat until chocolate is melted and sauce is smooth – do not overheat.

on the table in 10 minutes
serves 6
tip for a quick banana split, top sundae with half a banana cut into slices.

Rocky road topping

2 x 55g Cherry Ripe bars, chopped coarsely
50g mallow bakes
2 tablespoons crushed roasted peanuts
1 litre vanilla ice-cream
⅓ cup (80ml) chocolate Ice Magic

1 Combine Cherry Ripe, mallow bakes and nuts in medium bowl.
2 Spoon ice-cream into four serving bowls; top with Cherry Ripe mixture then drizzle with Ice Magic.

on the table in 5 minutes
serves 4

Mocha liqueur sundae

100g dark eating chocolate
⅔ cup (160ml) thickened cream
1 tablespoon Tia Maria
1 litre chocolate ice-cream
150g chocolate-coated coffee beans

1 Stir chocolate and cream in medium saucepan, over low heat, until mixture is smooth; stir in liqueur. Cool 10 minutes.
2 Layer ice-cream, chocolate sauce and coffee beans in four serving glasses.

on the table in 20 minutes
serve 4
tip Kahlúa can be substituted for Tia Maria.

Ice-cream with hot rhubarb sauce

500g chopped rhubarb
¾ cup (165g) caster sugar
½ cup (125ml) orange juice
1 litre vanilla ice-cream

1 Combine rhubarb, sugar and juice in medium saucepan; bring to a boil.
Reduce heat, simmer until rhubarb is soft.
2 Serve hot rhubarb sauce over ice-cream scoops.

on the table in 20 minutes
serves 4

Warm caramel sundaes

125g butter, chopped
300ml cream
1 cup (200g) firmly packed brown sugar
1 tablespoon cornflour
1 tablespoon water
500ml vanilla ice-cream
100g jersey caramels, chopped

1 Stir butter, cream and sugar in medium saucepan over low heat until butter is melted.
2 Stir in blended cornflour and water; bring to a boil. Simmer, uncovered, about 3 minutes or until thickened slightly.
3 Divide scoops of ice-cream among serving bowls, top with warm caramel sauce and with jersey caramels.

on the table in 20 minutes
serves 4

Ice-cream with espresso and irish cream

2 tablespoons finely ground espresso coffee
⅔ cup (160ml) boiling water
500ml vanilla ice-cream
½ cup (125ml) irish cream liqueur

1 Place coffee and the water in coffee plunger; stand 2 minutes, plunge coffee. Cool 5 minutes.
2 Divide ice-cream among serving glasses; drizzle with liqueur then coffee. Serve immediately.

on the table in 15 minutes
serves 4
tip we used Bailey's Irish Cream in the recipe, but you can use any irish cream liqueur.

DO AHEAD • The following recipes require refrigeration or freezing ahead of serving.

Watermelon sorbet

½ cup (125ml) water
½ cup (110g) caster sugar
850g coarsely chopped seedless watermelon
1 egg white

1 Stir the water and sugar in small saucepan over heat, without boiling, until sugar dissolves; bring to a boil. Reduce heat, simmer, uncovered, without stirring, 5 minutes; cool.
2 Meanwhile, blend or process watermelon until smooth; strain through fine sieve into sugar syrup. Stir to combine.
3 Pour sorbet mixture into shallow cake pan, cover with foil; freeze about 3 hours or until almost set.
4 Chop frozen watermelon mixture coarsely. Blend or process with egg white until smooth. Return mixture to pan, cover; freeze until firm.

• **preparation time** 15 minutes (plus freezing time)
cooking time 10 minutes (plus cooling time)
serves 4
tips you need a 1.2kg piece of watermelon for this recipe. You can also freeze the sorbet-egg white mixture in an ice-cream machine following the manufacturer's instructions.

Coco-cherry ice-cream timbale

2 litres vanilla ice-cream
2 x 85g Cherry Ripe bars, chopped coarsely
1 cup (140g) vienna almonds, chopped coarsely
50g pink marshmallows, chopped coarsely
50g dark eating chocolate, chopped coarsely
pink food colouring
300ml cream
100g white eating chocolate, chopped finely

1 Soften ice-cream in large bowl; stir in Cherry Ripe, nuts, marshmallow, dark chocolate and enough colouring to tint the ice-cream pink. Divide mixture among eight 1-cup (250ml) moulds. Cover with foil; freeze 3 hours or overnight.
2 Place cream in small saucepan; bring to a boil. Remove from heat; add white chocolate, stir until chocolate melts.
3 Turn ice-cream timbales onto serving plates; drizzle with warm white chocolate sauce.

• **preparation time** 10 minutes (plus refrigeration time)
cooking time 2 minutes
serves 8
tip use a good quality ice-cream; actual varieties of ice-cream differ from manufacturer to manufacturer depending on the quantities of air and fat incorporated into the mixture.

Coffee granita with walnut crisps

2 cups (500ml) boiling water
¼ cup (30g) ground coffee beans
⅓ cup (75g) caster sugar
walnut crisps
10g butter
1 tablespoon honey
1 tablespoon plain flour
1 tablespoon icing sugar
2 tablespoons finely chopped roasted walnuts

1 Pour the boiling water over coffee in small plunger; stand 5 minutes before plunging and pouring into medium jug. Add caster sugar; stir until sugar dissolves. Pour coffee into shallow cake pan, cover with foil; freeze about 3 hours or until almost set.
2 Using fork, scrape granita from bottom and sides of pan, mixing frozen with unfrozen mixture, cover; return to freezer. Repeat process every hour for about 4 hours or until large ice crystals form and granita has a dry, shard-like appearance.
3 Meanwhile, make walnut crisps.
4 Serve granita with walnut crisps.
walnut crisps melt butter with honey in small saucepan over low heat; stir in flour, icing sugar and nuts. Place walnut crisp mixture into small bowl, cover; refrigerate 1 hour. Preheat oven to 220°C/200°C fan-forced. Line oven trays with baking paper. Drop level teaspoons of the crisp mixture on trays about 10cm apart; bake, uncovered, about 3 minutes or until crisps are browned lightly. Remove from oven; cool 1 minute. Using spatula, lift crisps carefully and place over rolling pin to cool.

• **preparation time** 25 minutes (plus freezing time)
cooking time 10 minutes (plus cooling time)
serves 4

Frozen citrus yogurt pots

500g packaged cream cheese, softened
1 cup (220g) caster sugar
3 cups (800g) vanilla yogurt
1 tablespoon finely grated lemon rind
1 tablespoon finely grated lime rind
½ cup (125ml) orange juice
⅓ cup (80ml) lemon juice
2 tablespoons lime juice
orange food colouring
⅓ cup (25g) shredded coconut, toasted

1 Place a collar of foil around six ¾-cup (180ml) dishes; secure with string.
2 Beat cheese and sugar in medium bowl with electric mixer until smooth. Gradually add yogurt; beat until smooth. Stir in rinds, juices and enough food colouring to tint mixture pale orange.
3 Divide mixture among dishes. Cover loosely with plastic wrap; freeze overnight.
4 Remove pots from freezer; stand 5 minutes. Remove collars; press coconut around sides. Freeze 5 minutes before serving.

• **preparation time** 20 minutes (plus freezing time)
serves 6

Poached plums and nougat ice-cream

½ cup (125ml) rosé or red wine
2½ cups (625ml) water
⅓ cup (75g) white sugar
12 (1kg) small plums
nougat ice-cream
500ml vanilla ice-cream
150g almond nougat, chopped

1 Make nougat ice-cream.
2 Place wine, the water and sugar in large saucepan, cook, stirring, until sugar is dissolved. Bring to a boil, then boil, uncovered, 2 minutes. Reduce heat, add plums; simmer, covered with a round of baking paper, about 5 minutes or until plums are just tender. Transfer plums from pan to heatproof medium bowl.
3 Simmer syrup, uncovered, about 5 minutes, or until thickened slightly; pour over plums.
4 Peel plums and serve with ice-cream and syrup.
nougat ice-cream combine ice-cream and nougat in medium bowl. Freeze until required.

• **preparation time** 10 minutes (plus freezing time)
cooking time 15 minutes
serves 4

Passionfruit ice-cream

2 cups (500ml) milk
8 egg yolks
⅔ cup (150g) caster sugar
⅔ cup (160ml) passionfruit pulp
300ml thickened cream

1 Bring milk to a boil in medium saucepan; remove from heat.
2 Meanwhile, whisk egg yolks and sugar in medium bowl with electric mixer until creamy; gradually whisk into hot milk. Return to heat, stir over low heat, without boiling, until mixture thickens slightly.
3 Transfer to large heatproof jug or bowl, press plastic wrap over surface of custard; cool, refrigerate until cold.
4 Stir passionfruit into custard, then add cream.
5 Pour mixture into shallow cake pan, cover with foil; freeze about 3 hours or until almost set.
6 Beat coarsely chopped ice-cream in large bowl with electric mixer until smooth; return mixture to cake pan. Cover; freeze until firm.

preparation time 15 minutes (plus refrigeration and freezing time)
cooking time 10 minutes (plus cooling time)
serves 8
tip you can also freeze the ice-cream mixture in an ice-cream machine following the manufacturer's instructions.

Pink grapefruit granita with hazelnut wafers

1 cup (250ml) water
1 cup (220g) sugar
1 cup (250ml) fresh pink grapefruit juice
¼ cup (60ml) lemon juice
2 egg whites
hazelnut wafers
1 egg white
¼ cup (55g) caster sugar
2 tablespoons hazelnut meal
20g butter, melted

1 Stir the water and sugar in small saucepan over heat, without boiling, until sugar dissolves; bring to a boil. Boil, uncovered, without stirring, about 5 minutes. Remove from heat; stir in juices, cool to room temperature.
2 Beat egg whites in small bowl with electric mixer until soft peaks form. Fold grapefruit syrup into egg white mixture; pour sorbet mixture into shallow cake pan, cover with foil; freeze about 3 hours or until almost set.
3 Chop mixture coarsely. Blend or process until pale and creamy. Return mixture to pan, cover; freeze until firm.
4 Meanwhile, preheat oven to 180°C/160°C fan-forced. Grease two oven trays; line each with baking paper. Make hazelnut wafers.
5 Serve granita with hazelnut wafers.
hazelnut wafers beat egg white in small bowl with electric mixer until soft peaks form; gradually add sugar, beating until sugar dissolves between additions. Add hazelnut meal and butter; stir until combined. Trace 16 x 7cm circles, 2cm apart, on lined trays. Spread a teaspoon of mixture in each circle. Bake about 5 minutes or until lightly browned. Cool wafers on trays before carefully peeling away paper.

preparation time 20 minutes (plus freezing time)
cooking time 10 minutes
serves 8
tips you will need 2 large pink grapefruit for this recipe. You can also freeze the granita mixture in an ice-cream machine following the manufacturer's instructions.

Lemon sorbet

2½ cups (625ml) water
¼ cup finely grated lemon rind
1 cup (220g) caster sugar
¾ cup (180ml) lemon juice
1 egg white

1 Stir the water, rind and sugar in small saucepan over heat, without boiling, until sugar dissolves; bring to a boil. Boil, uncovered, without stirring, about 5 minutes or until syrup thickens slightly. Strain into medium heatproof jug; cool to room temperature. Stir in juice.
2 Pour sorbet mixture into shallow cake pan, cover with foil; freeze about 3 hours or until almost set.
3 Chop lemon mixture coarsely. Blend or process with egg white until smooth. Return mixture to pan, cover; freeze until firm.

● **preparation time** 15 minutes (plus freezing time)
cooking time 10 minutes (plus cooling time)
serves 4
tips you will need 4 lemons for this recipe. You can also freeze the sorbet-egg white mixture in an ice-cream machine following the manufacturer's instructions.

Frozen nectarine and turkish delight parfait

2 cups (400g) ricotta cheese
¾ cup (165g) caster sugar
300ml thickened cream
100g white chocolate Toblerone, chopped finely
100g turkish delight, chopped finely
1 cup (150g) chopped nectarines

1 Line 14cm x 21cm loaf pan with a strip of foil or baking paper to cover the base and extend over the two long sides.
2 Beat cheese and sugar in small bowl with electric mixer until smooth. Transfer mixture to large bowl.
3 Beat cream in small bowl with electric mixer until soft peaks form. Stir chocolate, turkish delight and nectarines into ricotta mixture; fold in cream.
4 Spoon mixture into pan, smooth top; cover, freeze overnight or until firm.
5 Turn parfait out onto board; slice. Stand at least 15 minutes or until softened slightly before serving. Decorate with extra chopped turkish delight, if desired.

● **preparation time** 20 minutes (plus freezing and standing time)
serves 6

Almond and raspberry frozen puddings

3 eggs
⅓ cup (75g) caster sugar
600ml thickened cream
1 teaspoon vanilla extract
1 tablespoon kirsch
⅓ cup (45g) vienna almonds, chopped coarsely
⅔ cup (70g) frozen raspberries
200g white eating chocolate, melted
fresh raspberries, for serving, optional

1 Beat eggs and sugar in small bowl with electric mixer about 5 minutes or until the mixture is very pale and fluffy. Transfer to large bowl.
2 Beat cream, extract and liqueur in clean small bowl with electric mixer until soft peaks form. Gently fold cream mixture into egg mixture along with nuts and frozen raspberries.
3 Divide mixture among six ¾-cup (180ml) moulds. Cover; freeze overnight or until firm.
4 Wipe moulds with hot damp cloth; turn out onto plates. Spoon melted chocolate over top. Serve with fresh raspberries and sprinkled with extra chopped vienna almonds, if desired.

• **preparation time** 25 minutes (plus freezing time)
serves 6

Grapefruit and campari granita

½ cup (110g) caster sugar
1 cup (250ml) water
2 tablespoons finely grated ruby red or pink grapefruit rind
1 litre (4 cups) ruby red or pink grapefruit juice, strained
½ cup (125ml) Campari

1 Stir sugar and the water in small saucepan over heat, without boiling, until sugar dissolves; bring to a boil. Boil, uncovered, without stirring about 5 minutes or until syrup thickened slightly, remove from heat; cool to room temperature. Stir in rind, juice and Campari.
2 Pour mixture into shallow cake pan, cover with foil; freeze about 3 hours or until almost set.
3 Using fork, scrape granita from bottom and sides of pan, mixing frozen with unfrozen mixture, cover; return to freezer. Repeat process every hour for about 4 hours or until large ice crystals form and granita has a dry, shard-like appearance.
4 Serve granita in individual serving glasses.

• **preparation time** 15 minutes (plus freezing time)
cooking time 10 minutes (plus cooling time)
serves 6

Rhubarb crumble ice-cream

2 cups (220g) chopped rhubarb
2 tablespoons brown sugar
2 litres vanilla ice-cream, softened slightly
125g Ginger Nut biscuits, chopped coarsely

1 Grease 14cm x 21cm loaf pan; line base and two long sides with foil or baking paper extending above edges of pan.
2 Cook rhubarb and sugar in large heavy-based saucepan, covered, about 5 minutes or until rhubarb is almost tender. Reduce heat, simmer, uncovered, about 5 minutes or until rhubarb softens but retains shape. Cool.
3 Place ice-cream in large bowl; break up slightly. Gently swirl in biscuits and rhubarb mixture.
4 Spoon ice-cream mixture into pan. Cover; freeze 3 hours or until firm.

preparation time 10 minutes (plus freezing time)
cooking time 10 minutes (plus cooling time)
serves 8

Chocolate nougat frozen parfait

2¼ cups (450g) ricotta cheese
½ cup (110g) caster sugar
200g dark eating chocolate, melted
150g almond nougat, chopped coarsely
300ml thickened cream

1 Grease 14cm x 21cm loaf pan; line base and two long sides with baking paper, extending paper above edges of pan.
2 Blend or process cheese and sugar until smooth; transfer to medium bowl. Stir in chocolate and nougat.
3 Beat cream in small bowl with electric mixer until soft peaks form. Fold cream into chocolate mixture.
4 Spoon mixture into pan, cover with foil; freeze overnight.
5 Remove parfait from pan; slice thickly. Stand 10 minutes before serving.

• **preparation time** 20 minutes (plus freezing time)
serves 8

Frozen passionfruit yogurt

½ cup (110g) caster sugar
¼ cup (60ml) water
1 teaspoon gelatine
2 cups (560g) yogurt
½ cup (125ml) passionfruit pulp

1 Stir sugar and the water in small saucepan, over low heat, until sugar dissolves; transfer to medium heatproof jug.
2 Sprinkle gelatine over sugar syrup, stirring until gelatine dissolves.
3 Combine yogurt and pulp in jug with syrup. Pour yogurt mixture into loaf pan, cover tightly with foil; freeze 3 hours or until almost set.
4 Scrape yogurt mixture from bottom and sides of pan with fork; return to freezer until firm.

● **preparation time** 10 minutes (plus freezing time)
cooking time 5 minutes
serves 4
tip you will need about 6 passionfruit for this recipe.

Raspberry sorbet

1 cup (250ml) water
1 cup (220g) caster sugar
600g frozen raspberries
1 tablespoon lemon juice
2 egg whites

1 Stir the water and sugar in small saucepan over heat, without boiling, until sugar dissolves; bring to a boil. Reduce heat, simmer, uncovered, without stirring, 5 minutes; cool.

2 Blend or process raspberries, juice and sugar syrup until smooth.

3 Push mixture through fine sieve into shallow cake pan; discard seeds. Cover with foil; freeze about 3 hours or until almost set.

4 Chop frozen berry mixture coarsely. Blend or process with egg whites until smooth. Return mixture to pan, cover; freeze until firm.

preparation time 15 minutes (plus freezing time)
cooking time 10 minutes (plus cooling time)
serves 6
tips raspberries may be replaced with any other berry. You can also freeze the sorbet-egg white mixture in an ice-cream machine following the manufacturer's instructions.

Choc crunch ice-cream with strawberries

1 litre vanilla ice-cream
8 Tim Tam biscuits, chopped coarsely
250g fresh strawberries, halved

1 Spoon ice-cream into medium bowl, stand 10 minutes to soften slightly.
2 Fold biscuits into ice-cream until just combined. Return ice-cream to container, cover; freeze until firm.
3 Serve ice-cream with strawberries.

• **preparation time** 10 minutes (plus freezing time)
  serves 4

Lemon and vodka sorbet

1 lemon
1 cup (220g) caster sugar
2½ cups (625ml) water
½ cup (125ml) lemon juice
¼ cup (60ml) vodka
1 egg white

1 Peel the rind thinly from lemon using a vegetable peeler. Cut the rind into long, thin strips. (Or, remove rind with a zester.)
2 Stir rind, sugar and the water in small saucepan over heat, without boiling, until sugar dissolves; bring to a boil. Reduce heat, simmer, uncovered, without stirring, about 5 minutes. Strain into medium heatproof jug; reserving rind. Cool to room temperature. Stir in juice and vodka
3 Pour mixture into shallow cake pan, cover with foil; freeze about 3 hours or until almost set.
4 Chop lemon vodka mixture coarsely. Blend or process with egg white until smooth. Return mixture to pan, cover; freeze until firm.
5 Serve sorbet topped with reserved rind in lemon shells, if desired.

• **preparation time** 15 minutes (plus freezing time)
cooking time 10 minutes (plus cooling time)
serves 6
tip to make the lemon shells, remove a small slice from the base of 6 lemons so they sit flat. Cut the tops and scoop out flesh and seeds with a teaspoon. Freeze on a tray until firm.

Nougat semifreddo with orange and honey syrup

1 vanilla bean
3 eggs, separated
⅓ cup (75g) caster sugar
1½ cups (375ml) thickened cream
200g almond nougat, chopped finely
½ cup (75g) coarsely chopped toasted shelled pistachios
1 tablespoon honey
orange honey syrup
¼ cup (90g) honey
1 tablespoon finely grated orange rind
2 tablespoons orange juice

1 Split vanilla bean in half lengthways; scrape seeds into small bowl, reserve pod for another use. Add yolks and sugar; beat with electric mixer until thick and creamy. Transfer mixture to large bowl.
2 Beat cream in small bowl with electric mixer until soft peaks form; gently fold cream into yolk mixture.
3 Beat egg whites in separate small bowl with electric mixer until soft peaks form. Gently fold half of the egg whites into cream mixture; fold in nougat, nuts, honey and remaining egg white. Transfer mixture to 14cm x 21cm loaf pan, cover with foil; freeze 3 hours or until just firm.
4 Meanwhile, make orange honey syrup.
5 Stand semifreddo at room temperature about 10 minutes before serving with syrup.
orange honey syrup place ingredients in small saucepan; bring to a boil. Reduce heat, simmer, uncovered, 2 minutes.

• **preparation time** 20 minutes (plus freezing time)
cooking time 5 minutes
serves 4

Raspberry toffee ice-cream cake

1 litre vanilla ice-cream
1 litre raspberry sorbet (or other fruit flavour)
1 litre English toffee ice-cream
240g fresh raspberries

1 Line deep 19cm square cake pan with foil or plastic wrap to cover base and extend over sides.
2 Soften vanilla ice-cream slightly. Evenly press mixture into pan. Freeze about 1 hour or until firm.
3 Evenly press sorbet over vanilla. Freeze about 1 hour or until firm.
4 Soften toffee ice-cream slightly, press over sorbet layer. Cover; freeze about 6 hours or overnight until firm.
5 Turn ice-cream cake onto serving platter; cover with raspberries. Serve immediately.

• **preparation time** 15 minutes (plus freezing time)
serves 12

Dried apricots in cardamom syrup with pistachio ice-cream

1 litre vanilla ice-cream, softened
⅔ cup (100g) coarsely chopped pistachios, toasted lightly
1⅔ cups (250g) dried apricots
2 cups (500ml) boiling water
¼ cup (55g) caster sugar
3 cardamom pods
1 cinnamon stick

1 Combine ice-cream and pistachios in medium bowl. Divide ice-cream mixture among eight ½ cup (125ml) moulds. Cover; freeze overnight or until firm.
2 Place apricots and the water in medium saucepan; stand 30 minutes.
3 Add sugar, cardamom pods and cinnamon stick to apricots; bring to a boil. Reduce heat, simmer, uncovered, about 10 minutes or until syrup is reduced by half. Cool 10 minutes.
4 Wipe ice-cream and moulds with a hot damp cloth and turn out onto serving plates. Serve with apricots and a little of the cardamom syrup.

• **preparation time** 15 minutes (plus freezing time)
cooking time 15 minutes (plus cooling time)
serves 8

Choc-chip nougat frozen parfait with caramel sauce

2 cups (400g) ricotta cheese
⅔ cups (150g) caster sugar
1⅓ cups (330ml) thickened cream
150g almond nougat, chopped
50g chopped dark eating chocolate
caramel sauce
1 cups (220g) caster sugar
⅔ cup (160ml) water
⅔ cup (160ml) thickened cream

1 Grease 9cm x 21cm loaf pan (base measurement); line base and two long sides with foil or baking paper extending above edges of pan.
2 Process cheese and sugar until smooth. Beat cream in small bowl with electric mixer until soft peaks form. Combine cheese mixture, nougat and chocolate in large bowl; fold in cream.
3 Spoon mixture into pan. Cover; freeze overnight or until firm.
4 Meanwhile, make caramel sauce.
5 Turn out parfait; cut into slices. Allow parfait to soften slightly before serving with caramel sauce.
caramel sauce stir sugar and the water in small saucepan, over low heat, until sugar is dissolved. Boil, uncovered, without stirring, until a caramel colour. Remove pan from heat, allow bubbles to subside. Carefully add cream, stir over low heat to dissolve the toffee. Cool.

preparation time 25 minutes (plus freezing time)
cooking time 10 minutes
serves 8

sauces

Rich caramel sauce

1 cup (220g) caster sugar
½ cup (125ml) water
300g thickened cream

1 Stir sugar and the water in small saucepan over low heat until sugar dissolves. Bring to a boil; boil, uncovered, without stirring, about 15 minutes or until mixture turns a caramel colour.
2 Remove from heat; allow bubbles to subside. Gradually add cream, stirring constantly, over low heat, until sauce is smooth. Cool 10 minutes.

on the table in 35 minutes
makes 1½ cups
tip goes well with apple pie, grilled bananas, apple teacake or sticky date pudding.

White chocolate, coconut and orange sauce

⅔ cup (160g) cream
10cm strip orange rind
2 cardamom pods, bruised
180g white eating chocolate, chopped coarsely
2 teaspoons Malibu

1 Place cream, rind and cardamom in small saucepan; bring to a boil. Remove from heat.
2 Add chocolate and liqueur; stir until smooth. Strain sauce; discard cinnamon and rind.

on the table in 15 minutes
makes 1 cup
tips a citrus-flavoured liqueur, such as Grand Marnier, can be substituted for the Malibu, if you prefer. Goes well with poached plums, peaches or ice-cream.

Choc-mallow sauce

4 x 60g Mars Bars, chopped finely
300ml cream
100g packet marshmallows

1 Stir Mars Bars and cream in small saucepan, over low heat, until smooth.
2 Add marshmallows, stir until smooth.

on the table in 20 minutes
makes 2 cups
tips replace Mars Bars with other chocolate bars such as Snickers or
Bounty. Liqueur can be added to create a different flavour, if desired.
Goes well with chocolate cake, apple pie or as a fondue with fruit.

Hazelnut cream

⅔ cup (160ml) cream
1 tablespoon Frangelico
1 tablespoon caster sugar
⅓ cup (45g) coarsely chopped roasted hazelnuts

1 Beat cream, liqueur and sugar in small bowl with electric mixer until soft peaks form; stir nuts into sauce.

on the table in 20 minutes
makes 1 cup
tip goes well with cold or warm cakes, puddings or sweet crepes.

Strawberry coulis

300g frozen strawberries, thawed
1 tablespoon icing sugar

1 Blend or process berries until smooth, push through fine sieve into small bowl; discard seeds. Stir sifted icing sugar into sauce.

on the table in 10 minutes
makes 1 cup
tips any berries, fresh or frozen, can be used. Other fruits such as mango, passionfruit, kiwifruit, and even guava or pineapple, can be used. Sugar needs to be adjusted according to the fruit used. Goes well with puddings, slices or poached fruits.

Coffee liqueur sauce

¼ cup (60ml) cream
⅔ cup (160ml) freshly brewed strong coffee
250g white eating chocolate, chopped coarsely
1 tablespoon Tia Maria

1 Stir cream and coffee in small saucepan over medium heat, without boiling, until hot. Remove from heat; add chocolate, whisk until smooth. Stir in liqueur.
2 Transfer sauce to small bowl; cover, refrigerate about 15 minutes, stirring occasionally.

on the table in 35 minutes
makes 2 cups
tip goes well with pancakes, over waffles or as a fondue.

Orange butterscotch sauce

½ cup (125ml) thickened cream
½ cup (110g) firmly packed brown sugar
60g cold butter, chopped
1 teaspoon finely grated orange rind

1 Stir ingredients in small saucepan over low heat, without boiling, until sugar dissolves. Bring to a boil. Reduce heat; simmer, uncovered, 3 minutes.

on the table in 15 minutes
makes 1 cup
tip goes well with pancakes, waffles, warmed sponge cake, sweet crepes or poached oranges.

glossary

allspice also known as pimento or jamaican pepper; so-named because it tastes like a combination of nutmeg, cumin, clove and cinnamon. Available whole (a dark-brown berry the size of a pea) or ground, and used in both sweet and savoury dishes.

almonds flat, pointy-tipped nuts having a pitted brown shell enclosing a creamy white kernel which is covered by a brown skin.

flaked paper-thin slices.

meal also known as ground almonds; nuts are powdered to a coarse flour texture for use in baking or as a thickening agent.

scorched chocolate coated whole almonds.

slivered small pieces cut lengthways.

vienna toffee-coated almonds.

amaretti biscuits small Italian-style macaroons (biscuit or cookie) made with ground almonds.

baking powder a raising agent consisting mainly of two parts cream of tartar to one part bicarbonate of soda (baking soda).

bicarbonate of soda also known as baking soda; a mild alkali used as a leavening agent in baking.

breadcrumbs, stale crumbs made by grating, blending or processing 1- or 2-day-old bread.

brioche French in origin; a rich, yeast-leavened, cake-like bread made with butter and eggs. Most common form is the brioche à tête, a round fluted roll topped with a much smaller ball of dough. Eaten freshly baked or toasted; available from cake or specialty bread shops.

butter we use salted butter unless stated otherwise; 125g is equal to 1 stick (4oz) in other recipes. Unsalted or "sweet" butter has no added salt.

buttermilk in spite of its name, buttermilk is actually low in fat, varying between 0.6 per cent and 2.0 per cent per 100 ml. Originally the term given to the slightly sour liquid left after butter was churned from cream, today it is intentionally made from no-fat or low-fat milk to which specific bacterial cultures have been added during the manufacturing process. It is readily available from the dairy department in supermarkets. Because it is low in fat, it's a good substitute for dairy products such as cream or sour cream in some baking and salad dressings.

cardamom a spice native to India and used extensively in its cuisine; can be purchased in pod, seed or ground form. Has a distinctive aromatic, sweetly rich flavour and is one of the world's most expensive spices. Used to flavour curries, rice dishes, sweet desserts and cakes.

cheese

cream commonly known as philadelphia or philly; a soft cow-milk cheese with a fat content ranging from 14 per cent to 33 per cent.

mascarpone an Italian fresh cultured-cream product made in much the same way as yogurt. Whiteish to creamy yellow in colour, with a buttery-rich, luscious texture. Soft, creamy and spreadable, it is used in many Italian desserts and as an accompaniment to a dessert of fresh fruit.

ricotta a soft, sweet, moist, white cow-milk cheese with a low fat content (about 8.5 per cent) and a slightly grainy texture. The name roughly translates as "cooked again" and refers to ricotta's manufacture from a whey that is itself a by-product of other cheese making.

cherry small, soft stone fruit varying in colour from yellow to dark red. Sweet cherries are eaten whole and in desserts while sour cherries such as the morello variety are used for jams, preserves, pies and savoury dishes.

chocolate

dark eating also known as semi-sweet or luxury chocolate; made of a high percentage of cocoa liquor and cocoa butter, and little added sugar. Unless stated otherwise, we use dark eating chocolate in this book as it's ideal for use in desserts and cakes.

ice magic a quick setting chocolate sauce available from most supermarkets.

melts small discs of compounded milk, white or dark chocolate ideal for melting and moulding.

white contains no cocoa solids but derives its sweet flavour from cocoa butter. Very sensitive to heat.

chocolate hazelnut spread also known as Nutella.

cinnamon available both in the piece (called sticks or quills) and ground into powder; one of the world's most common spices, used universally as a sweet, fragrant flavouring for both sweet and savoury foods. The dried inner bark of the shoots of the Sri Lankan native cinnamon tree; much of what is sold as the real thing is in fact cassia, Chinese cinnamon, from the bark of the cassia tree. Less expensive to process than true cinnamon, it is often blended with Sri Lankan cinnamon to produce the type of "cinnamon" most commonly found in supermarkets.

cloves dried flower buds of a tropical tree; can be used whole or in ground form. They have a strong scent and taste so should be used sparingly.

cocoa powder also known as unsweetened cocoa; cocoa beans (cacao seeds) that have been fermented, roasted, shelled, ground into powder then cleared of most of the fat content. Unsweetened cocoa is used in hot chocolate drink mixtures; milk powder and sugar are added to the ground product.

coconut

cream obtained commercially from the first pressing of the coconut flesh alone, without the addition of water; the second pressing (less rich) is sold as coconut milk. Available in cans and cartons at most supermarkets.

flaked: dried flaked coconut flesh.

milk not the liquid found inside the fruit, which is called coconut water, but the diluted liquid from the second pressing of the white flesh of a mature coconut (the first pressing produces coconut cream). Available in cans and cartons at most supermarkets.

shredded unsweetened thin strips of dried coconut flesh.

coconut macaroons made from coconut, egg white and cornflour.

cornflour also known as cornstarch. Available made from corn or wheat (wheaten cornflour, gluten-free, gives a lighter texture in cakes); used as a thickening agent in cooking.

crème de cacao chocolate-flavoured liqueur.

crème fraîche a mature, naturally fermented cream (minimum fat content 35 per cent) having a velvety texture and slightly tangy, nutty flavour. Crème fraîche, a French variation of sour cream, can boil without curdling and can be used in both sweet and savoury dishes.

custard powder instant mixture used to make pouring custard; similar to North American instant pudding mixes.

dates fruit of the date palm tree, eaten fresh or dried, on their own or in prepared dishes. About 4cm to 6cm in length, oval and plump, thin-skinned, with a honey-sweet flavour and sticky texture. Best known, perhaps, for its inclusion in sticky toffee pudding; also found in muesli and other cereals; muffins, scones and cakes; compotes and stewed fruit desserts.

egg we use large chicken eggs having an average weigh of 60g in our recipes unless stated otherwise. If a recipe calls for raw or barely cooked eggs, exercise caution if there is a salmonella problem in your area.

figs are best eaten in peak season, at the height of summer. Vary in skin and flesh colour according to type not ripeness: the purple-black mission or black mission fig, with pink flesh, is a rich-flavoured, good all-rounder; the thick-skinned, pale green kadota, another all-purpose fruit, is good canned or dried as well as fresh; the yellow smyrna has nutty-tasting flesh; and the pale olive, golden-skinned adriatic has honey-sweet, light pink flesh. When ripe, figs should be unblemished and bursting with flesh; nectar beads at the base indicate when a fig is at its best.

flour

plain also known as all-purpose; unbleached wheat flour is the best for baking.

rice very fine, almost powdery, gluten-free flour; made from ground white rice. Used in baking, as a thickener, and in some Asian noodles and desserts.

self-raising all-purpose plain or wholemeal flour with baking powder and salt added; can be made at home with plain or wholemeal flour sifted with baking powder in the proportion of 1 cup flour to 2 teaspoons baking powder.

wholemeal also known as wholewheat flour; milled with the wheat germ so is higher in fibre and more nutritional than white flour.

gelatine we use dried (powdered) gelatine in the recipes in this book; it's also available in sheet form known as leaf gelatine. A thickening agent made from either collagen, a protein found in animal connective tissue and bones, or certain algae (agar-agar). Three teaspoons of dried gelatine (8g or one sachet) is roughly equivalent to four gelatine leaves.

ginger

crystallised sweetened with cane sugar.

fresh also known as green or root ginger; the thick gnarled root of a tropical plant. Can be kept, peeled, covered with dry sherry in a jar and refrigerated, or frozen in an airtight container.

glacé fresh ginger root preserved in sugar syrup; crystallised ginger can be substituted if rinsed with warm water and dried before using.

ground also known as powdered ginger; used

as a flavouring in cakes, pies and puddings but cannot be substituted for fresh ginger.

wine, green a beverage that is 14% alcohol by volume, has the piquant taste of fresh ginger.

golden syrup a by-product of refined sugarcane; pure maple syrup or honey can be substituted. Golden syrup and treacle (a thicker, darker syrup not unlike molasses), also known as flavour syrups, are similar sugar products made by partly breaking down sugar into its component parts and adding water. Treacle is more viscous, and has a stronger flavour and aroma than golden syrup.

hazelnuts also known as filberts; plump, grape-size, rich, sweet nut having a brown inedible skin that is removed by rubbing heated nuts together vigorously in a tea-towel. Hazelnut meal is made by grounding the hazelnuts to a coarse flour texture.

honeydew melon a heavy oval fruit with a pale-green to yellow skin, delicate taste and pale green flesh.

instant pudding mix a blancmange-style dessert mix.

jam also known as preserve or conserve; a thickened mixture of a fruit (and occasionally, a vegetable) and sugar.

jam rollettes we used 9cm long sponge rolls filled with jam or jam and cream; these are generally purchased in 250g packets of six.

kaffir lime also known as magrood, leech lime or jeruk purut. The wrinkled, bumpy-skinned green fruit of a small citrus tree originally grown in South Africa and South East Asia. As a rule, only the rind or leaves are used.

kaffir lime leaves also known as bai magrood, look like they are two glossy dark green leaves joined end to end, forming a rounded hourglass shape. Used fresh or dried in many South East Asian dishes, they are used like bay leaves or curry leaves, especially in Thai cooking. Sold fresh, dried or frozen, the dried leaves are less potent so double the number if using them as a substitute for fresh; a strip of fresh lime peel may be substituted for each kaffir lime leaf.

kiwifruit also known as Chinese gooseberry; having a brown, somewhat hairy skin and bright-green flesh with a unique sweet-tart flavour. Used in fruit salads, desserts and eaten (peeled) as is.

lemon grass also known as takrai, serai or serah. A tall, clumping, lemon-smelling and tasting, sharp-edged aromatic tropical grass; the white lower part of the stem is used, finely chopped, in much of the cooking of South East Asia. Available fresh, dried, powdered and frozen, in supermarkets, greengrocers and Asian food shops.

lychees a small fruit from China with a hard shell and sweet, juicy flesh. The white flesh has a gelatinous texture and musky, perfumed taste. Discard the rough skin and seed before using in salads or as a dessert fruit. Also available canned in a sugar syrup.

macadamias native to Australia; fairly large, slightly soft, buttery rich nut. Should always be stored in the fridge to prevent their high oil content turning them rancid.

maple syrup distilled from the sap of sugar maple trees found only in Canada and about ten states in the USA.

Most often eaten with pancakes or waffles, but also used as an ingredient in baking or in preparing desserts. Maple-flavoured syrup or pancake syrup is not an adequate substitute for the real thing.

maple-flavoured syrup is made from sugar cane and is also known as golden or pancake syrup. It is not a substitute for pure maple syrup.

marsala a fortified Italian wine produced in the region surrounding the Sicilian city of Marsala; recognisable by its intense amber colour and complex aroma.

milk we use full-cream homogenised milk unless otherwise specified.

sweetened condensed a canned milk product consisting of milk with more than half the water content removed and sugar added to the remaining milk.

mixed peel candied citrus peel.

mixed spice a classic mixture generally containing caraway, allspice, coriander, cumin, nutmeg and ginger, although cinnamon and other spices can be added. It is used with fruit and in cakes.

muesli also known as granola; a combination of grains (mainly oats), nuts and dried fruits.

nashi a member if the pear family but resembling an apple with its pale-yellow-green, tennis-ball-sized appearance; more commonly known as the Asian pear to much of the world. The nashi is different from other pears in that it is crisp, juicy and ready to eat as soon as it is picked and for several months thereafter, unlike its European cousins.

nougat a popular confection in southern Europe; made from sugar or honey, roasted nuts, sometimes candied fruits and beaten egg white (for soft nougat) or caramelised sugar (for hard nougat).

nutmeg a strong and very pungent spice ground from the dried nut of an evergreen tree native to Indonesia. Usually found ground but the flavour is more intense from a whole nut, available from spice shops, so it's best to grate your own. Found in mixed spice mixtures.

orange flower water concentrated flavouring made from orange blossoms.

papaya the papaya family includes both the yellow-fleshed fruit called pawpaw and the pink-fleshed fruit called papaya. Their milky, sweet flavour is best with a squeeze of lime.

peanut butter peanuts ground to a paste; available in crunchy and smooth varieties.

pecans native to the US and now grown locally; pecans are golden brown, buttery and rich. Good in savoury as well as sweet dishes; walnuts are a good substitute.

pepitas the pale green kernels of dried pumpkin seeds; available plain or salted.

pistachios green, delicately flavoured nuts inside hard off-white shells. Available salted or unsalted in their shells; you can also get them shelled.

poppy seeds small, dried, bluish-grey seeds of the poppy plant, with a crunchy texture and a nutty flavour. Can be purchased whole or ground in most supermarkets.

rambutan a relative of the lychee, with similar luscious, perfumed, grape-like flesh. To remove the leathery, tendril-covered shell, break open with a fingernail and peel like an egg.

ready-rolled puff pastry packaged sheets of frozen puff pastry, available from supermarkets.

saffron threads stigma of a member of the crocus family, available ground or in strands; imparts a yellow-orange colour to food once infused. The quality can vary greatly; the best is the most expensive spice in the world.

savoiardi sponge finger biscuits also known as savoy biscuits, lady's fingers or sponge fingers; Italian-style crisp fingers made from sponge cake mixture.

star anise a dried star-shaped pod whose seeds have an astringent aniseed flavour; commonly used to flavour stocks and marinades.

starfruit also called arombola and belimbing (a smaller variety). Some ripen to yellow or pinky yellow, most to a yellow-green. Very crisp and juicy, with a mild sweet flavour.

sugar we use coarse, granulated table sugar, also known as crystal sugar, unless otherwise specified.

brown an extremely soft, fine granulated sugar retaining molasses for its characteristic colour and flavour.

caster also known as superfine or finely granulated table sugar. The fine crystals dissolve easily so it is perfect for cakes, meringues and desserts.

cinnamon combination of ground cinnamon and caster sugar. Most commonly sprinkled over buttered toast.

icing also known as confectioners' sugar or powdered sugar; pulverised granulated sugar crushed together with a small amount (about 3 per cent) of cornflour.

palm also known as nam tan pip, jaggery, jawa or gula melaka; made from the sap of the sugar palm tree. Light brown to black in colour and usually sold in rock-hard cakes; substitute with brown sugar if unavailable.

raw natural brown granulated sugar.

sunflower seeds grey-green, slightly soft, oily kernels; a delicious and nutritious snack.

tequila colourless alcoholic liquor of Mexican origin made

from the fermented sap of the agave, a succulent desert plant.

vanilla

bean dried, long, thin pod from a tropical golden orchid grown in central and South America and Tahiti; the minuscule black seeds inside the bean are used to impart a luscious vanilla flavour in baking and desserts. Place a whole bean in a jar of sugar to make the vanilla sugar often called for in recipes.

bean paste a convenient paste made from vanilla beans.

essence obtained from vanilla beans infused in alcohol and water.

extract obtained from vanilla beans infused in water; a non-alcoholic version of essence.

vinegar, balsamic originally from Modena, Italy, there are now many balsamic vinegars on the market ranging in pungency and quality depending on how, and for how long, they have been aged.

yogurt we use plain full-cream yogurt unless otherwise specified. If a recipe in this book calls for low-fat yogurt, use one with a fat content of less than 0.2 per cent.

index

MEASURES

One Australian metric measuring cup holds approximately 250ml, one Australian metric tablespoon holds 20ml, one Australian metric teaspoon holds 5ml.

The difference between one country's measuring cups and another's is within a two- or three-teaspoon variance, and will not affect your cooking results.North America, New Zealand and the United Kingdom use a 15ml tablespoon.

All cup and spoon measurements are level. The most accurate way of measuring dry ingredients is to weigh them. When measuring liquids, use a clear glass or plastic jug with the metric markings.

We use large eggs with an average weight of 60g.

LIQUID MEASURES

METRIC	IMPERIAL
30ml	1 fluid oz
60ml	2 fluid oz
100ml	3 fluid oz
125ml	4 fluid oz
150ml	5 fluid oz (¼ pint/1 gill)
190ml	6 fluid oz
250ml	8 fluid oz
300ml	10 fluid oz (½ pint)
500ml	16 fluid oz
600ml	20 fluid oz (1 pint)
1000ml (1 litre)	1¾ pints

LENGTH MEASURES

METRIC	IMPERIAL
3mm	⅛in
6mm	¼in
1cm	½in
2cm	¾in
2.5cm	1in
5cm	2in
6cm	2½in
8cm	3in
10cm	4in
13cm	5in
15cm	6in
18cm	7in
20cm	8in
23cm	9in
25cm	10in
28cm	11in
30cm	12in (1ft)

DRY MEASURES

METRIC	IMPERIAL
15g	½oz
30g	1oz
60g	2oz
90g	3oz
125g	4oz (¼lb)
155g	5oz
185g	6oz
220g	7oz
250g	8oz (½lb)
280g	9oz
315g	10oz
345g	11oz
375g	12oz (¾lb)
410g	13oz
440g	14oz
470g	15oz
500g	16oz (1lb)
750g	24oz (1½lb)
1kg	32oz (2lb)

OVEN TEMPERATURES

These oven temperatures are only a guide for conventional ovens.
For fan-forced ovens, check the manufacturer's manual.

	°C (CELSIUS)	°F (FAHRENHEIT)	GAS MARK
Very slow	120	250	½
Slow	150	275 – 300	1 – 2
Moderately slow	160	325	3
Moderate	180	350 – 375	4 – 5
Moderately hot	200	400	6
Hot	220	425 – 450	7 – 8
Very hot	240	475	9

Editorial director Susan Tomnay
Creative director Hieu Chi Nguyen
Food director Pamela Clark
Food editor Louise Patniotis
Senior editor Stephanie Kistner
Designer Caryl Wiggins
Director of sales Brian Cearnes
Marketing manager Bridget Cody
Business analyst Ashley Davies

Chief executive officer Ian Law
Group publisher Pat Ingram
General manager Christine Whiston
Editorial director (WW) Deborah Thomas

WW food team Lyndey Milan, Alexandra Elliott, Frances Abdallaoui

Produced by ACP Books, Sydney.
Printing by Toppan Printing Co., China.
Published by ACP Books, a division of ACP Magazines Ltd,
54 Park St, Sydney; GPO Box 4088, Sydney, NSW 2001
phone +61 2 9282 8618 fax +61 2 9267 9438
acpbooks@acpmagazines.com.au www.acpbooks.com.au
To order books phone 136 116 (within Australia)
Send recipe enquiries to recipeenquiries@acpmagazines.com.au

RIGHTS ENQUIRIES
Laura Bamford, Director ACP Books
lbamford@acpuk.com

Australia Distributed by Network Services,
phone +61 2 9282 8777 fax +61 2 9264 3278
networkweb@networkservicescompany.com.au
United Kingdom Distributed by Australian Consolidated Press (UK),
phone (01604) 642 200 fax (01604) 642 300
books@acpuk.com
New Zealand Distributed by Netlink Distribution Company, phone (9) 366 9966
ask@ndc.co.nz
South Africa Distributed by PSD Promotions,
phone (27 11) 392 6065/6/7 fax (27 11) 392 6079/80
orders@psdprom.co.za

Clark, Pamela.
Fast desserts
ISBN 978-1-86396-654-2
1. Desserts. 2. Cookery (Puddings).
I. Title. II. Title: Australian women's weekly.
641.86
© ACP Magazines Ltd 2007
ABN 18 053 273 546

Cover Almond and raspberry frozen puddings, page 349
Photographer Louise Lister
Stylist Stephanie Souvlis
Food preparation Ariarne Bradshaw